STILL LIFE AT THE POETRY CAFE

The Poetry Season

4 Penguin Modern Poets: Carol Ann Duffy, Eavan Boland, Peter Reading, Glyn Maxwell, Blake Morrison, Kit Wright, Vicki Feaver; the original volumes

14 Louis MacNeice: Jon Stallworthy's biography reviewed by Peter Forbes

17 John Betjeman's 'Business Girls' with illustration by David Gentleman

18 Elizabeth Bartlett interviewed by Carol Rumens; poem by Elizabeth Bartlett

23 Poem by Sophie Hannah; her first collection reviewed by John Whitworth

25 Poems by James Berry, Kate Clanchy, Lawrence Sail, Roger Crawford, Bernard O'Donoghue

29 Helen Dunmore on first collections; the Poetry Season – highlights

32 Ted Hughes reviewed by Don Paterson

Poetry & Science

34 Leon Cych and Chris Meade on the Internet; poem by Jackie Hardy;

40 Paul Mills: The Quantum Uncertainty of the Narrator; poems by Pascale Petit, Sally Carr, Keki N. Daruwalla, Amanda Wilson, John Goodby, John Latham, Lavinia Greenlaw, Peter Howard, William Scammell, John Burnside

54 Peter Redgrove's Incubator; poem by Maurice Riordan

Poetry & Health

58 Dr Robin Philipp and Mike Sharpe on the therapeutic effects of poetry; poem by Marion Lomax

The Poetry Season

61 Swansea UK Year of Literature and Writing: poems by Gwyneth Lewis, Deryn Rees-Jones, Jean Earle; Ian McMillan on Deryn Rees-Jones, Catherine Fisher and Tim Liardet; poems by Kathy Miles, Paul Groves, John Powell Ward, Paul Henry

68 The Classic Poem: Dannie Abse chooses Bernard Spencer's 'Part of Plenty'

Reviews & Poems

69 Michael Donaghy on Marilyn Hacker; poem by Alice Friman, Martyn Crucefix on David Harsent; Robert Crawford on Iain Crichton Smith; poem by E. A. Markham; Anthony Rudolf on Carolyn Forché; Dennis O'Driscoll on Harry Smart; poem by Ian Gregson

78 David Constantine's *Caspar Hauser* reviewed by Michael Hulse; poem by Atar Hadari, John Bayley on Christopher Logue; Laurie Smith on Peter Porter, Michael Horovitz on Ginsberg; Roger Garfitt on C. H. Sisson, Peter Levi, Thomas Lynch, Stuart Henson, Neil Powell, Neil Curry

88 Poem by Carol Rumens; Sean O'Brien on Edna Longley; David Kennedy on Deborah Randall; poem by John Gohorry

Endstops

92 Letters, Competition Report, Back numbers

Cover illustration by Brian Gallagher

…ume 85
Number 1

CONTENTS

Editor
Peter Forbes

Society needs Poetry: *JOIN the* Poetry Society

If you write, read, teach or promote poetry, join the Society to develop your knowledge and enjoyment of Britain's most buoyant and participatory artform.

You Will Receive ...

POETRY NEWS. Our new look quarterly newsletter packed with opportunities, ideas and comment. Special issues and supplements will focus on poetry and education, libraries, festivals and new writers.

POETRY REVIEW, Britain's leading poetry magazine: 'essential reading for anyone who wants to keep up to date with new poetry. It's the magazine which readers of poetry can't do without.' **– Douglas Dunn, Whitbread Prize Winner**

Discounts On ...

THE NATIONAL POETRY COMPETITION. This is open to all – with thirteen cash prizes totalling £5,250 – and has built up a remarkable track record for discovering new talent and affirming the reputations of established names. Past prizewinners include Tony Harrison, Carol Ann Duffy, and Jo Shapcott. 1993's winner, Sam Gardiner, was a newcomer to poetry, unknown – until he won £3,000 and saw his poem published by the *Guardian*.

THE SCRIPT, a unique service to all those who write poetry. Fill out a questionnaire specially devised to help you think about how and why you write, then send it in with a sample of your poetry for a 'diagnosis' from a skilled professional poet and a 'prescription' of new ideas and further reading.

POETRY READINGS, talks and events around the UK.

INFORMATION & IMAGINATION: seminars, fact sheets, training courses for teachers, librarians, promoters, poets and all those who love poetry.

HELPING POETRY THRIVE IN BRITAIN TODAY

MEMBERSHIP RATES

UK Individuals	£24	☐
UK Concessionary rate (Pensioners, Students, UB40)	£18	☐
UK Institutions	£30	☐
European Union	£30	☐
Rest of world (surface)	£30	☐
" " (airmail)	£40	☐
Life membership (UK only)	£250	☐
Poetry Review only	£20	☐

Tachers/students: Please tick if you want to be included on the Education mailing list ☐

I wish to make a donation to the Poetry Society of
£10 ☐ £20 ☐ £50 ☐ £100 ☐

I enclose a cheque for £________
Please debit my Access/Visa account
expiry date________
Card No.

Name ________

Address________

Please send coupon to:
Membership Secretary, Poetry Society,
22 Betterton St, London WC2H 9BU

PHOTOCOPY THIS FORM

Still Life at the Poetry Cafe

The long-term effects of last year's media bonanza for poetry are slowly coming to light. One is that there is now a real sense of the poetry season, with a succession of major prizes. We felt we should help this on its way by drawing attention to forthcoming publishing highlights, hence the Poetry Season listing on p.31 The Poetry Society's main contribution to the Season will be the Christmas Poetry Catalogue, to be launched in the Autumn alongside a special issue of the *Review* focusing on the reading of poetry. It was very noticeable that after poetry's *annus mirabilis*, it still dropped off the map during the Christmas book promotions. This year it will be a little bit harder to ignore poetry.

The last time poetry was truly popular, every student seemed to have a copy of Penguin Modern Poets nos 5 and 10 (if you don't remember which they were, see p.13). Now, emboldened by New Generation Poets and National Poetry Day, Penguin are relaunching the idea, with three volumes of three poets apiece appearing in May.

Another major arrival this year is the Swansea UK Year of Literature. One of its aims is to highlight Welsh writing, and it is unfortunately true that Welsh poetry has been unlucky recently. Some of the most interesting young poets, like Gwyneth Lewis and Deryn Rees-Jones, did not yet have a book at the time of New Generation and therefore were not contenders. We are pleased to be able to highlight some of these poets now.

'Poetry-and-Science' is very much on the menu at the moment, but it has to be said that much of the interest could be the result of a basic misunderstanding. Paul Mills's article on page 40 expounds the Standard Model for a new relationship between poetry and science: that there is a convergence between scientific and postmodern notions of reality: that the Uncertainty Principle in physics is a metaphor for the unreliability of texts. A long time ago, W. C. Williams came to a similar conclusion re Relativity: ie that conventional metrics could be equated with Newtonian Mechanics, whereas *his* prosody registered the cosmic shift of Einsteinian Relativity. Williams and Mills are wrong. The technical terms Relativity and the Uncertainty Principle have nothing to do with the everyday use of the words. Physics is largely a matter of mathematical symbolisation and much of it cannot be paraphrased in words. Loose analogies may excite poets but they betray the science absolutely. Primo Levi, in the story 'Potassium' from *The Periodic Table*, said: 'We must distrust the almost the same'. Poets should take heed.

The wild card this year is the Internet: the Poetry Society arrived in cyberspace in February. At the moment, waiting long minutes for graphics files to download must be very like the experience of a former generation listening to early crystal sets: it's magnificent but also pretty awful. But the potential is obvious to see. For *Poetry Review* it will give a much-needed stimulus towards indexing and creating an interactive magazine. It is shameful to admit it, but *Poetry Review* has never been indexed. A typical problem: The cross-referencing of Peter Howard's poem on page 51 to the Lavinia Greenlaw poem it is based on proved difficult: without an index, the editor's memory is the only retrieval aid, and there were no clues other than that it had appeared somewhere between Autumn 1990 and Spring 1994. Compare that to the possibility of a hypertext *Poetry Review* in which, when you click on a poet's name, all of that poet's poems and reviews of their work will come up on screen. At present when we get requests from researchers for all of Derek Walcott's or Peter Redgrove's pieces in *PR*, the heart sinks. Soon it will be child's play. At present such useful things are not on the Net, but the Net is not what is there now, but what is about to be put on it. The Internet is at least a useful bibliographical tool and information resource. It will not circumvent existing editorial procedures, and it will not replace a printed *Poetry Review*, but the élan of the idea of it is something we welcome very much. **PF**

Penguin Modern Poets Relaunch

The original Penguin Modern Poets series ran to 27 volumes from 1962 to 1979. The first three volumes of the new series launched in May feature: JAMES FENTON, KIT WRIGHT, BLAKE MORRISON; EAVAN BOLAND, CAROL ANN DUFFY, VICKI FEAVER; MICK IMLAH, GLYN MAXWELL, and PETER READING. To celebrate we asked the poets for new poems and/or a brief reminiscence of the original series.

CAROL ANN DUFFY

Mrs Quasimodo's Divorce

I'd loved them fervently since childhood.
Their generous bronze throats
gargling, then chanting slowly, calming me –
the village runt, name-called, stunted, lame, hare-lipped;
but bearing up, despite it all, sweet-tempered, good at needlework;
an ugly cliché in a field,
pressing dock-leaves to her fat, stung calves
and listening to the five cool bells of evensong.
I believed that they could even make it rain.

The city suited me; my lumpy shadow
lurching on its jagged alley walls;
my small eyes black
as rained-on cobblestones.
I frightened cats.
I lived alone up seven flights,
boiled potatoes on a ring
and fried a single silver fish;
then stared across the grey lead roofs
as dusk's blue rubber rubbed them out,
and then the bells began.

I climbed the belltower steps,
out of breath and sweating anxiously, puce-faced,
and found the campanologists beneath their ropes.
They made a space for me,
telling their names,
and when it came to him
I felt a thump of confidence,
a recognition like a struck match in my head,
and caught a sex smell coming from him,
coming my way.
It was Christmas-time.
The tusk that snagged his upper lip was wet with spit.
When the others left,

he fucked me underneath the gaping, stricken bells
until I wept.

We wed.
He swung an epithalamium for me,
embossed it on the fragrant air.
Long, sexy chimes,
exuberant peals,
slow scales trailing up and down the smaller bells,
an angelus.
We had no honeymoon,
but spent the week in bed.
And did I kiss
each part of him –
that horseshoe mouth,
that tetrahedron nose,
that squint left-eye,
that right eye with its pirate wart,
the salty leather of that pigs-hide throat,
and give his cock
a private name –
or not?

So more fool me.

We lived in the Cathedral grounds.
The bellringer.
The hunchback's wife.
The Quasimodos. Have you met them? Gross.
And got a life;
our neighbours – sullen gargoyles, fallen angels, cowled saints
who raised their marble hands in greeting
as I passed along the gravel paths,
my husband's supper on a tray beneath a cloth.
But once,
one evening in the Ladychapel on my own,
throughout his ringing of the seventh hour,
I kissed the cold lips of a King next to his Queen.
Don't ask me why.
Something had changed,
or never even been.
Soon enough,
he started to find fault.
Why did I this?
How could I that?
Look at myself.
And in that summer's dregs,
I'd see him
watch the pin-up gypsy with her goat

dancing for the tourists in the square;
then turn his discontented, traitor's eye on me
with no more love than stone.

I should have known.

Because it's better, isn't it, to be well-formed.
Better to be slim, be slight,
your slender neck quoted between two thumbs;
and beautiful, with creamy skin,
and tumbling auburn hair,
those devastating eyes;
and have each lovely foot
held in a gentle hand
and kissed;
then be watched till morning as you sleep,
so perfect, vulnerable and young
you hurt his blood.

And given sanctuary.

But not betrayed.
Not driven to an ecstasy of loathing of yourself;
banging your ugly head against a wall,
gaping in the mirror at your heavy dugs,
your thighs of lard,
your mottled upper arms;
thumping your belly –
look at it –
your wobbling gut.
You pig. You stupid cow. You fucking dog.
Abortion. Cripple. Spastic. Mongol. Ape.

Where did it end?
A ladder. Heavy tools. A steady hand.
And me, alone all night up there,
bent on revenge.
He had pet-names for them.
Marie.
The belfry trembled when she spoke for him.
I climbed inside her with my claw-hammer, my pliers, my saw, my clamp;
and, though it took an agonizing hour,
ripped out her brazen tongue
and let it fall.
Then Josephine,
his second-favourite bell,
kept open her astonished golden lips

and let me in.
The bells. The bells.
I made them mute.
No more arpeggios, or scales, no stretti, trills
for christenings, weddings, great occasions, happy days.
No more practising
for bellringers on smudgy autumn nights.
No clarity of sound, divine, articulate,
to purify the air
and bow the heads of drinkers in the city bars.
No single
solemn
funeral note
to answer
grief.

I sawed and pulled and hacked.
I wanted silence back.

Get this –

when I was done,
and bloody to the wrist,
I squatted down among the murdered music of the bells
and pissed.

Carol Ann Duffy writes:

I think it was about 1969, when I was 13, when I bought my first Penguin Modern Poets paperback. The poets were Corso, Ferlinghetti and Ginsberg and the price was half-a-crown - very affordable out of the proceeds of my Saturday job. Over the next three years I'd regularly buy either a PMP selection or – somehow more glamorous – one of the Penguin Modern European Poets. My favourites at the time were Prévert, Rilke, the Beats, the Liverpool lot, and the one with Stevie Smith in it. I also liked Jeff Nuttall's selection. Oh, the lost, intense happiness of walking over the railway bridge in the rain, with a new Penguin anthology, to Jane and Alice's house. I'm glad Penguin are doing them again.

Eavan Boland writes:

The new issues of Penguin Modern Poets were available when I was a young poet in Dublin in ways that other volumes of poetry weren't. I still remember their colour and black headlines and reading the spines with interest and excitement. That's where I first came on Denise Levertov. That's where I expected to find new poets and new poetry within a price range which excluded the risk that you wouldn't like them or might not want to keep them. The great value and romance of the volumes then has to be set against the relative enclosure and claustrophobia of each poetic village, one set off against the other by barriers of travel and communication and poor distribution. I knew almost nothing about the difference between West Coast poetry in the States or the New York school or indeed who was writing well in London or Manchester. These volumes opened a window and gave every young poet, and a great number of interested readers, the chance to see the vitality and range of tones, voices and initiatives that were happening in the poetic world.

PETER READING

Lucretian

[Only pain, not oblivion, hurts.]
Since the mind, like the body, is mortal,
death doesn't matter a toss.
When the brain and the carcass are severed,
we, who shall then be nothing,
can be troubled by nothing at all.

If we have ever existed
in any previous state,
we *now* know nothing about it;
so, when we snuff it, we won't
feel deprived of the present.

If, after death, there were dearth,
then the mind would have to be present
to experience deprivation;
but death, which denies the existence
of thought, exempts us from this.

One who no longer *is*
can't suffer – is merely the same
as one who has never been.

In sleep, neither mind nor body
feels itself 'absent' or craves life.
Extend this repose to eternity –
no sense of loss can obtain.

Prolonging life doesn't reduce
the duration of death, for the time
after departure is infinite –
non-being lasts just as long
for those who expire today
as it does for defunct Eolithics.

Peter Reading writes:

The first volume of the Penguin Modern Poets series which I remember contained work by George Barker, Martin Bell and Charles Causley. I bought a copy when I was an art student in the sixties and strutted about with it during rest breaks from the life-drawing class. Probably I encountered Timothy Winters and Johnny Alleluia there, but I am unable to remember this because the purpose of owning the book was to impress upon my peers and superiors the fact that I had literary pretentions. I believe that the cover of this volume showed a photograph of the seed pods of Honesty (Lunaria annua), *presumably to remind us of the aspiration of poetry to be truthful. I was a poseur/poetaster in those days and, thirty years later, I still am.*

GLYN MAXWELL

The Night is Young

I was with some friends when I noticed with some strangers
One of the Gang. And we rose like we'd won awards,
Reluctant and delighted, to a position
Halfway between our tables, and began,
Began with a tale of now and ourselves, but soon
Were hurrying back in the years like children yelled
Out of the light of their inexplicable game,
Into the brooding houses to be held.

Nothing's changed, we said, since everything had.
Again some time, we agreed, as it never would.
When I sipped and caught him searching my eyes for the kind
I was, he caught me searching his for the same.

Though my new friends and his, from time to time,
Would look across and point out a seat in the ring
For either stranger, no, we remained right there,
Steadily finishing off what was there to be said,
Drinking and putting our tankards down slowly.

And when there was nothing, listing the names like somehow
They'd be around us, the Gang, like the night there was no one
Missing. Weren't we over there by the window?

I'd seen some, but he'd seen two I expected
Never to see again, they were fine, they were fine,
He mentioned. and that was that.
                                        I returned to my circle,
Shaking him off as doubtless he shook me off,
Answering who he was with an oh someone,
Settling to the night, uncomfortable, gruff,
And feeling about as young as the night is young,
And wanting it all, like one who has had enough.
You don't forgive what's left of what you loved.

Glyn Maxwell writes:

I really am too young. All I remember is the neatness of the spines, the orderliness of the colours, wondering if each poet liked being with the other two. I thought it would make a lovely collection, but I'm not a collector.

Besides the Penguin selection, Gyn Maxwell had a new collection,* Rest for the Wicked, *published by Bloodaxe in March.

Blake Morrison writes:

In 1973, returning from a year in Canada and the US, I decided to become a poet. I'd been a poet before, but that had been mere child's play; now I went about the business seriously and – beginning with an impenetrable (even to me) piece of Yeatsiana composed on board the SS Estonia between Quebec and Southampton – went on to produce some of the worst juvenilia the world has never seen. I made every mistake a young poet of that time could make, including sending handwritten hommages à *Sylvia Plath to A. Alvarez at the* Observer *and thinking that Larkinesque resignation was the true elegiac note. It was a chastening apprenticeship.*

The only useful bit was the reading I did. My knowledge of poets since the Second World War was seriously limited, and I set about consuming as much as I could on a student grant. I remember being ejected from a bookshop in Blackheath after reading most of my way through the just-out High Windows. *But there were back-shelves at Compendium in Camden High Street, and even at Foyles, with dust-rich bargains. Most important, there was the Penguin Modern Poets series, which seemed the best, or at any rate cheapest, way of acquiring a quick knowledge of what contemporary poets were up to. I had volume 10 already, as everyone did, but now I hunted out the rest. It says something for publishing practice then that in 1975 I was buying editions that had been kept in print, or had at any rate stayed around, since 1967.*

1979 brought the end of the series, however: those garish red lips on the cover of volume 25 (Ewart-Ghose-B.S.Johnson) had signalled a loss of nerve, and there were only two more volumes. It's always narked me that I was never able to find Vol 19 (Ashbery-Harwood-Raworth), and looking at my shelves now I see that Vol 5 (Corso-Ferlinghetti-Ginsberg: surely the most interesting volume of the lot) has also gone missing. But if the bibliophile in me was denied, I think I also learnt an invaluable lesson: that there was more to contemporary poetry than Faber (or Lowell and Larkin). There will always be dud volumes in a series like this, but it was brave of Penguin to do, say, Jackson-Nuttall-Wantling, or Elmslie-Koch-Schuyler, and I hope the new series will be as receptive to different kinds of poetry as its predecessor was.

KIT WRIGHT
Rudy

Hoping to lose my way
In order at last to find it,
I lit out into the city canyons
Of faces half-remembered
From somewhere I'd never been,

And I followed for the hell of it
Whatever I'd not quite had in mind
To the outskirts and the dripping wood
Of the hurricane-slain beeches.
Birds were already at work

In the wrenched-out cavities, up
At each looming base and the dark rain
Had its fingers through the vents
In the canopy when I saw him
Leaning against the barrel

Of a felled oak. *O I was war*
Of a man in blak and the wood
Kept seeping and rustling as I moved
In spite of my life to meet him
In the sprawling brushwood. I

Had fallen one step short
Of travelling through his eyes
When I saw this was Ontario, more than
Half my life ago.
I am teaching Wordsworth's windy epiphanies

Over the air conditioning. Here
Has to be a grape-picker
From Beamsville or Vineland or Jordan
I drank with in the Mansion House
Hotel at twenty-two.

Chris, he says. I am listening
Only to him in the freezing timber
That must be the pine escarpment
High over the lunch-pail town. Chris?
And he tells me how it all went wrong

In Sakatchewan, how the prairie
Wind blew it all away.
Rudy, his name was. Rudy.
Christ, I see he is standing
Deader than hell in the pinewood, he

Whose love had come to nothing
In the whirling snow. If I could
Get us away from here. If I could
Drag us on to the highway, but it is
Dark beyond dark already,

Already way, way too late. *Rudy?*

TWO POEMS BY VICKI FEAVER

Bed

What in a fire I'd most want to save –
not watching, like Anne Bradstreet,
my household goods in flames,
and writing a poem of loss
attributing all to God,
but entering the smoke
before I can be stopped.
The house burns like a marriage
leaving black grease and ash.
The bed I bring out intact:
its brass coils loosening
and falling apart, the quilt's
bold zigzags, stitched from strips
of brilliant red, and cream flower-
printed cloth, frayed with use.
Bed where I embrace aloneness
whose limbs are any shape I want;
where I make, in the envelope
of crisp, soap-scented sheets,
in the only way I know,
(except for the rarer fall
of laundered snow), again and again
a new world; where, in the corridor
that leads between me and the sun,
I see, lit up, in the firmament
of dust, the debris of my skin
and broken hairs, rising
and falling on the air.

Anne Bradstreet (c.1612-1672), who sailed from England as a founding member of the Massachussetts Bay Company and became America's first poet, wrote 'Some Verses Upon the Burning of our House, July 10th, 1666'.

Glow Worm

Talking about the chemical changes
that make a body in love shine,
or even, for months, immune to illness,
you pick a grub from the lawn
and let it lie on your palm – glowing
like the emerald burning butt
of a cigarette. (We still haven't touched;
only lain side by side
the half stories of our half lives.)
You call them lightning bugs
from the way the males gather in clouds

and simultaneously flash.
This is the female, fat from a diet
of liquified snails, at the stage in her cycle
when she hardly eats; when all her energy's
directed to drawing water and oxygen
to a layer of luciferin.
Wingless, wordless,
in a flagrant and luminous bid
to resist the narrative's pull to death,
she lifts her shining green abdomen
to signal *yes yes yes*.

Vicki Feaver writes:

I've got about half the first Penguin Modern Poets series: a wedge of distinctive black paperbacks on my poetry shelves. They were a wonderful taster for someone who was just beginning to be interested in modern poetry. But I note now, with amazement, that among seventy-five poets only four were women. The work of three of these, Elizabeth Jennings, Denise Levertov and Stevie Smith, I've gone on to collect and read more and more. Stevie Smith, I actually went to hear – at the Morden Tower in Newcastle. Wearing a green wool dress with a white lace collar, she looked like a gawky grown-up child performing at a party. Yet listening to her off-key chanting, accompanied by a hissing gas fire, I got such a sense of conviction and authenticity, I came away reinforced with the idea of wanting to be a poet. What so appealed to me about her poems, and still does, is the way she mixes the magical and practical, and her anarchic play with language and 'the tradition', and the use she makes of myths and fairytales and the collective store of female wit and fantasy. It's thanks to her, and to Levertov and Jennings, and to all the other original and courageous women poets, before and after, who have challenged the myth of the poet as male, that the new Penguin series will be, richly and diversely, a balanced collection of men and women. I am so proud to be one of them.

The original series of Penguin Modern Poets ran from 1962 to 1979. The volumes were:

1 Lawrence Durrell, Elizabeth Jennings, R.S. Thomas.
2 Kingsley Amis, Dom Moraes, Peter Porter
3 George Barker, Martin Bell, Charles Causley
4 David Holbrook, Christopher Middleton, David Wevill
5 Alan Ginsberg, Gregory Corso, Lawrence Ferlinghetti
6 Jack Clemo, Edward Lucie-Smith, George MacBeth
7 Richard Murphy, Jon Silkin, Nathaniel Tarn
8 Edwin Brock, Geoffrey Hill, Stevie Smith
9 Denise Levertov, Kenneth Rexroth, William Carlos Williams
10 Adrian Henri, Roger McGough, Brian Patten
11 D.M. Black, Peter Redgrove, D.M. Thomas
12 Alan Jackson, Jeff Nuttall, William Wantling
13 Charles Bukowski, Phillip Lamantia, Harold Norse
14 Alan Brownjohn, Michael Hamburger, Charles Tomlinson
15 Alan Bold, Edward Brathwaite, Edwin Morgan
16 Jack Beeching, Harry Guest, Matthew Mead
17 David Gascoigne, W.S. Graham, Kathleen Raine
18 A. Alvarez, Roy Fuller, Anthony Thwaite
19 John Ashbery, Lee Harwood, Tom Raworth
20 John Heath-Stubbs, F.T. Prince, Stephen Spender
21 Iain Crichton Smith, Norman MacCaig, George Mackay Brown
22 John Fuller, Peter Levi, Adrian Mitchell
23 Geoffrey Grigson, Edwin Muir, Adrian Stokes
24 Kenneth Elmslie, Kenneth Koch, James Schuyler
25 Gavin Ewart, Zulfikar Ghose, B.S. Johnson
26 Dannie Abse, Michael Longley, D.J. Enright
27 Jon Ormond, Emrys Humphreys, John Tripp

The Miller of Hell

Peter Forbes on the first biography of Louis MacNeice

Jon Stallworthy,
Louis MacNeice,
Faber, £20
ISBN 0 571 160190
Louis MacNeice,
Selected Plays,
edited by Alan Heuser and Peter McDonald,
Clarendon Press, £35
ISBN 0 19 811245 9

'One at a time there! One at a time! Rotten oats on the left, mildewed barley on the right! .....I'll buy all your doubts and disappointments, your defeated hopes, your encumbrances, I'll buy all your chares and your chores, your backbitings and your second thoughts. Come on up there, shovel them in – your hypocrisies and mediocrities, your outmoded ornaments and armaments, your half-baked lumps of dough, your half-formed castles in the air, your stillborn babies, your unhappy pasts...bring it all up and shovel it in, it's grist to my mill and to hell with it!'
('The Mad Islands')

MacNeice was a man who saw through things: saw through the fashionable nostrums peddled by his contemporaries, the embracing of the Proletariat, the cult of technical excellence, the child cult, the cult of sex ('Every woman her own harlot'). He was also a more desperate man than the urbane surface of his work suggests.

At the heart of Jon Stallworthy's biography is a four-and-a-half page (in print) 1939 letter to his then girlfriend Eleanor Clarke. Far removed from the insouciantly mannered prose of MacNeice's autobiography, *The Strings Are False* ('flower beds planted from bright, gay, intelligent seeds out of labelled packets' – Stephen Spender), it reveals the damaged childhood that leaks into so many poems, and also the source of that unillusioned vision:

> If in one's childhood one has had to act as interpreter for an idiot brother whom none of the adults could understand, if one has been kept awake half the night every night by a father moaning about his life, if one has got so that one winces in advance on behalf of one's family's reactions in any possible situation, the important effect is not the (admittedly heavy) effect on one's nerves but the terrifying, precocious development of insight.

To see clearly the follies of the age is valuable, but MacNeice is doubly precious because this insight did not make him a nihilist. His writing is shot through with affirmations: 'In spite of analytical researches into the pathology of sainthood, the saint, like the mathematician, has got hold of something positive. And so have the real hero and the real artist' (*The Strings are False*). The litany of 'The Good' remains pretty constant throughout his career, being most explicit in *Autumn Journal* and 'The Kingdom': work, the natural world, scholarship, courage, endurance, above all, women.

Sexual love looms large in this biography. Beyond his work, MacNeice's life was largely his love-life. A man who lost his mother at the age of seven and whose first wife left him after seven years of marriage might justifiably claim to have a deficit to make up. Add that MacNeice had a highly developed aesthetic of the moment as the ultimate good to fling in the face of drudgery, tedium and the cant of ideologues – and the fact that he was the best love poet of the century, with a requirement for muses– and you have a potent cocktail.

MacNeice seems to have married his first girlfriend. Mary was so vividly described in *The Strings are False* that the one photograph of her in the book is a grave disappointment. Supposedly an impossibly frail, fey creature, she is shown, with her borzoi, looking hefty and capable of running a farm (which she later did, in America). After Mary, MacNeice went on a binge – '1937 for me was a year of wild sensations' – but there don't seem to have been many one-night stands. MacNeice believed in love: 'the tangles' as he called it. 'Leaving Barra', 'Les Sylphides', 'Trilogy for X', 'September has come, and I wake' from *Autumn Journal*, above all 'Meeting Point' – MacNeice was the first poet of modern love (and the first poet was the best poet): frankly sexual – his women were not etherealized into the Pre-Raphaelite wraiths the Victorians swooned over (except perhaps Mary for a time, and she was his first).

It is the epiphanies of love that MacNeice seizes in his poetry, its 'bright fantasia' casting a glow on the surroundings. 'The camels crossed the miles of sand' in 'Meeting Point' must be one of the oddest romantic lines in poetry, but it is also one of the best, conveying effortlessly the imaginative expansion, the Baudelairean out-of-this-world quality of intensely focused love.

MacNeice began his sexual quest looking for 'the Not Impossible She'. But of course she was impossible: she was the mother he never had. His second marriage, though, to the singer Hedli Andersen, a vivacious redhead, seems to have been happy until ruined by MacNeice's drinking. There were more tangles in MacNeice's last years.

The principal scenes of MacNeice's life are already well known from *The Strings are False* (which goes up to 1940), Barbara Coulton's *Louis MacNeice in the BBC* (1941 to his death in 1963), and various memoirs by friends and acquaintances such as Nancy Coldstream, Geoffrey Grigson, Dan Davin and Margaret Gardiner. The reader familiar with these sources will mostly be fascinated by the detailed unravelling of MacNeice's love life. But the book is written with the new reader in mind.

Accounts of MacNeice by those who knew him are contradictory in a way that is hardly resolved by this book. Many testify to his gaiety, his relish for experience, people, conversation and sport. But just as many refer to his aloofness, his silence on social occasions. His work is shot through with images of stasis, petrifaction, sterile automatism. When he began to write, the dialectic was clear: reacting against the gloom of a Presbyterian childhood, with a dying mother, an idiot bother, and a tormented preacher of a father, he espoused everything that was 'high coloured....up-to-date'. But this was a facile reaction that was not going to get him very far.

Birmingham made MacNeice. He came there at the age of 23 after formative years at Marlborough and Oxford being trained as an English intellectual snob, and discovered there an everyday world where he felt 'reassurance in silent gardeners, in inefficient hospital nurses, in a golfer cupping his match in his hands in the wind, in business men talking shop in the train'. But note that there is still something of the *poseur* in this. MacNeice isn't like these people: they quicken his sensibility; by being other, they are more interesting than the intellectuals in their goldfish bowls (which is how he saw them), endlessly rebreathing the same depleted air. In Birmingham the dandy and the average sensual man began to engage in a dialectic in his poetry, sometimes in the obviously divided form of the Eclogue, at other times trading lines, as in 'Ode'.

There is no doubt that from this time on he adhered faithfully to a wary kind of humanism. He became supremely skilled at articulating the voice of the man in the street, though he never pretended he was that man. So he celebrates, 'the routine courage of the worker', the lives of those for whom holiday *joie de vivre* is 'contraband', 'the brown lace sinking in the glass of stout'. He wrote of sport and pubs and popular entertainment. His famous recipe for the modern poet – 'I would have the poet able-bodied, fond of talking, a reader of the newspapers, capable of pity and laughter, informed in economics, appreciative of women, involved in personal relationships, actively interested in politics, susceptible to physical impressions' – was a self-portrait and one he remained true to.

So much has been talked about MacNeice and Auden, MacNeice and Ireland: Peter McDonald says, in his book *Louis MacNeice: the Poet in his Contexts* (Clarendon Press, 1991): 'the difficulties from which MacNeice's reputation has always suffered have their origin in his poetic violation of certain canonical (and contextual) norms: a 1930s poet who insisted on his Irishness; an Irish-born poet who lived most of his life in England'. The idea is that somehow we couldn't see him for Auden's shadow; that he had to be reclaimed as a Northern Irish poet following the eclipse of his reputation in England after his death. But a look at his best poems shows what evasive nonsense this is. You don't need 'Auden' or 'Ulster' to interpret 'Snow', 'Morning Sun', 'Meeting Point', 'The Brandy Glass', 'The Cyclist', 'Star Gazer', 'Soap Suds'. They are poems of vivid moments, of the 'toppling wave' of the present. They are not date-bound or culture–bound – any intelligent reader – not even necessarily a regular reader of poetry – would understand them instantly. Their kinship is with Shakespeare's sonnets, Keats's Odes, and Hopkin's inscape, if literary precedents are needed, but more importantly they are written in the conversational language of the 20th century, to heightened effect certainly, but the emotions are instantly recognizable. What all the talk about contexts reveals is that many people are terrified of looking at poems without maps, and that they prefer politics and polemic to poetry – something which is inimical to the spirit of MacNeice.

It is true that some of his poems deal specifically with his Irish background and that *Autumn Journal*, his masterpiece, is both a key 30s text – and hence to a small degree indebted to Auden– and eloquently concerned with his contexts, but again the poems speak perfectly directly about these things: there is no interpretative lens through which they need to be viewed for their quality to become apparent.

MacNeice's own account of his life to the age of

thirty-three is a masterpiece: what does this Life add? Jon Stallworthy's biography could not be more different from Andrew Motion's Larkin. Stallworthy remains courteous, protective of both his subject and those who were close to him. It is a generous book, in keeping with MacNeice's own nature. But at time you feel that Stallworthy is *too* protective and often simply incurious. An unfortunate tendency in the book is to regurgitate chunks of *The Strings are False* without even a twist of paraphrase or alternative viewpoint. Thus, MacNeice's account of his engagement: 'One day, aided by rum and the Mozart Horn Concerto, I found myself engaged to Mariette' [in the book he calls Mary Mariette]. Stallworthy: 'One day, encouraged by rum and a Mozart Horn Concerto, he found himself engaged to her'. At a deeper level, Stallworthy's assumption that readers won't know the poetry reduces the value of what he can say about the poems in relation to the life.

Given that Stallworthy shrinks from exposing MacNeice's weaknesses, it seems only right to attempt it here. MacNeice inspires great devotion in his admirers (among whom I yield to none), but we might do our hero a service by acknowledging aspects that could be offputting to some. Jon Stallworthy does mention MacNeice's early intellectual snobbery. It does not seem to me so much snobbery as an irritating repertoire of affectations (on going down from Oxford, he wrote to Anthony Blunt: 'To get a first is a mistake, I have never been so afflicted with ennui'). He had a weakness for cliché, which at best he turned into a philosophy of sacraments in the poem 'Homage to Clichés', but it also led to him littering his work with automatic French tags such as *'Qu'allais-je faire dans cette galère?'*, which clearly was talismanic for him but comes over as a pat shrug of disdain. He was too fond of *qua* and *à la*. His introductions to the plays and *Autumn Journal* have a whiff of immodesty, and one anecdote in the book bears this out – at a lunch party given by John Betjeman, B. found him 'gauche, literary & irritating as ever. I was obviously expected to mention his poetry but abstained from doing so'. He never seemed to doubt that poetically and intellectually he was a fine fellow, with an assured entrée into Fabers, the BBC, the British Council etc. But worst of all was his schmalzy acceptance of the Fitzrovia boozing myth. Slopping from one drinking club to another and boasting that you've been drinking round the clock is the kind of imbecility that he was usually the first to see through. He did write some wonderful poems about drink, but of course the best drunken poem, 'Snow', isn't about alcohol at all. I suppose one has to assume that he stepped up his intake when he found he couldn't write any more poems like 'Snow'. By the time he was writing brilliantly again – the parable poems of his last two books, the booze was on automatic delivery. Jon Stallworthy is unhappy with the idea that MacNeice was an alcoholic at the end of his life. He puts it down to 'the BBC way of life'. As a hack's euphemism this could replace 'tired and emotional' but it won't do.

MacNeice's's radio work is often blamed for the fall off in his poetry during the 40s and 50s. But the radio plays are a significant part of his *oeuvre.* He joined the BBC in 1941 and the broad canvas he employed in *Autumn Journal* henceforth appeared only in his radio plays (*Autumn Sequel* was the exception but that remains a resounding clinker). MacNeice was a natural magnet for myths, and radio gave this side of him full rein. *Selected Plays* prints seven out of his seventeen radio plays, plus the stage play *One for the Grave. Christopher Columbus, The Dark Tower,* and *The Mad Islands* should be read by anyone who loves the poetry. The last play, *Persons from Porlock,* is an uncanny work: it killed him, sending him down a cave to record sound-effects, and it ends with the death of an artist. In between it rehashes so many of MacNeice's key themes, it's hard to resist the idea that something in him knew what was coming.

It was horribly appropriate that the cave killed him: MacNeice's life had a shape – the forces of petrifaction he could talk lightly about in his 20s hardened and grew colder. Joy could bubble up in poems like 'Snow' and 'Leaving Barra', but by the early 50s the poems were weakened by stale automatic responses. His love of cliché both in art and life was a dangerous balancing act. So the bravado of 'Homage to Clichés' – 'what'll you have my dear, the same again' – became a death warrant. The same again had weakened him so much that when he went into the cave to record effects for *Persons from Porlock,* the chill he caught became pneumonia.

MacNeice's work speaks to us even more resonantly now because the condition of being a displaced person has become the norm. He intelligently assessed the consolations available in a post-religious world, and what he discovered remains true, and seems likely to for a long time to come. His work is a casebook of how to live provisionally, without comforting myths of religion or nationality – how to juggle the competing claims the world and people make on us, how to reconcile make-believe and brute fact, how to love and hate the world to which we for a time belong.

The llustrated Betjeman

John Betjeman's publishers have become adept at attractively repackaging the most popular English poet of the 20th century. Now we have effectively a Selected Poems with illustrations by David Gentleman. Given Betjeman's topographical interests and his association with John Piper, Gentleman is an astute choice as illustrator. In case anyone has forgotten, Betjeman was one of the few modern poets to write equally well about people and things. In his best poems he weds his architectural obsessions to his human concerns.

JOHN BETJEMAN

Business Girls

From the geyser ventilators.
  Autumn winds are blowing down
On a thousand business women
  Having baths in Camden Town.

Waste pipes chuckle into runnels,
  Steam's escaping here and there,
Morning trains through Camden cutting
  Shake the Crescent and the Square.

Early nip of changeful autumn,
  Dahlias glimpsed through garden doors,
At the back precarious bathrooms
  Jutting out from upper floors;

And behind their frail partitions
  Business women lie and soak,
Seeing through the draughty skylight
  Flying clouds and railway smoke.

Rest you there, poor unbelov'd ones,
  Lap your loneliness in heat.
All too soon the tiny breakfast,
  Trolley-bus and windy street!

The Illustrated Poems of John Betjeman, ***with watercolours by David Gentleman, is published on April 20th by John Murray, £17.95, ISBN 0 7195 5248 6***

Strange Territory: Elizabeth Bartlett Interviewed

Elizabeth Bartlett's Selected Poems,* Two Women Dancing, *was published by Bloodaxe in February. Carol Rumens interviewed her, by post, in Spring 1994.

Carol Rumens: *You come from a working-class background, English and Irish. Could you tell us a little more about this?*

Elizabeth Bartlett: This 'working-class background' stuff bothers me sometimes. Yes, it was working class, and it was poor, but it wasn't typical. All my father's sisters and brothers became teachers and two went to university, but, as the eldest, he missed out on this and after a spell in the regular army he became a grocer's assistant. The Irish connection is just one grandmother who came to England as a child, but she was the mother of all these clever children. My father could well have been a pedantic teacher, but spent his leisure time writing out his life in red exercise books with a stub of pencil and urging his children on to win scholarships and educate ourselves.

CR: *Were you a bookish child? How soon did you feel you would become a writer? Was this ambition encouraged?*

EB: I was a bookish child and enlisted under-age at the public library. I'm still a pretty bookish old lady spending more time reading than doing other things. I always thought I would be a writer, but writing novels like *Jane Eyre*, not poetry. Nobody except my mother would have discouraged me and I aimed to have a red exercise book as soon as I could.

CR: *Your work has an air of self-confidence. Does this reflect in any way a feeling that being from a non-literary background and missing out on further education were not actually disadvantages, but even gains?*

EB: I don't know about the self-confidence bit. As you can see, the 'non-literary background' is a bit of a myth anyway and I've been going to WEA classes and Centre for Continuing Education groups for nearly forty years, which is probably as useful as the usual three year degree course. Perhaps 'the air of self-confidence' is more to do with being sure of what it is you want to do, whether you fail or not.

CR: *In your work, is its social dimension aimed at effecting possible political change? Do you believe poetry could make something happen?*

EB: No, I don't believe poetry can effect possible political change. Poetry does make things happen, but not in this way. I certainly never intended to be primarily a 'social' poet, although, yet again, I seem to see that my active Socialist father may have unwittingly indoctrinated me for life.

CR: *Is the sick or oppressed person also a metaphor for the poet in contemporary society?*

EB: As far as I know the 'sick and oppressed person' isn't 'also a metaphor for the poet in contemporary society'; or not in my poems. Perhaps Peter Reading might claim this. For me, it was what was close to hand to write about, part of daily life observed, shocking, necessary to expose in a way. This is the kind of intellectual argument I try to avoid most of the time. Was *The Waste Land* what the critics said? Eliot said: 'Various critics have done me the honour to interpret the poem in terms of criticism of the contemporary world, have considered it, indeed, as an important bit of social criticism. To me, it was only the relief of a personal and wholly insignificant grouse against life; it is just a piece of rhythmical grumbling'.

CR: *Do you feel in any way connected to a later generation of working-class poets, including such writers as Tony Harrison and Douglas Dunn, for example?*

EB: Not really. I admire Harrison, and Dunn, but 'connected' is not quite the word. I don't know a lot about Dunn, but Harrison's father was probably more truly working-class than mine. Well, no red exercise book for a start.

CR: *Do you think poetry has been harmed by poets writing self-consciously for the academic, lit-crit market? What are your views on the poet's place in the academy?*

EB: The only way in which poetry is ever harmed is when a certain falsity is so evident even the lit crit market is not fooled. All poetry is self-conscious to a certain extent. A certain stance is something one can't really avoid, much though one would like to sometimes.

CR: *There seems to be a notion in England that being from the south-east and being working-class are somehow incompatible. It you're not northern or 'regional' you must be 'metropolitan' and toffee-nosed. (This infuriates me!) Does it annoy you?*

EB: Not much about class and the North/South divide annoys me any more. I guess that fifty years in the middle class, by virtue of marriage, have made me appear to be one of them. So far, all my publishers have been Northern and they haven't made me feel unwelcome, and certainly not toffee-nosed. I suspect that what you say is true, but anyone who thinks Burgess Hill is metropolitan just because of the south-east voice couldn't be more wrong.

CR: Who were your first poetic influences, and who are your favourite poets now?

EB: Well, Rupert Brooke of course, at school, and then, mercifully, all the war poets, Owen and Sassoon in particular and Edward Thomas. This was the set syllabus for 1935, dubbed Modern Poetry, and made a great impact on me. I graduated, after marriage at nineteen, to Eliot and Rilke, partly because my husband brought me books and copies of *Poetry London* when he came on leave. He was a writer of short stories and, later, novels. Fortunately, only a few poems survive from the 1940s, although 'Half Holiday' which was published in *Poetry London* is included in the new book because I was beginning to write in a quite different way from the teenage poems – not much of Rupert Brooke in this poem.

My favourite poets now are still Edward Thomas and Owen, also Hardy, Eliot and more recently Lowell, Peter Porter, Judith Wright, but what really interests me is the work of women poets like Carol Ann Duffy, Jackie Kay, Fleur Adcock, Sylvia Kantaris, Carole Satyamurti, Connie Bensley, yourself and so many others. For women poets it's a very exciting time and it was one hell of a long time coming.

Elizabeth Bartlett was born in 1924. She worked as a medical secretary for 16 years and later in the Home Help Service. Her first collection,* A Lifetime of Dying: Poems 1942-1979*, was published by Peterloo in 1979. Since then there have been four collections:* Strange Territory *(Peterloo, 1983),* The Czar is Dead *(Rivelin-Grapheme, 1986),* Look, No Face *(Redbeck Press, 1991), and* Instead of a Mass *(Headland, 1993).* Two Women Dancing: New & Selected Poems *(Bloodaxe, £8.95, ISBN 15224 297 3) will be reviewed by Carol Ann Duffy in the next issue

CR: 'At first, like a new toy, I was played with, seduced ....'. This seems to be a description of your treatment as a newly emergent poet. If so, tell us more about this. Was it destructive at the time?

EB: This seems like a mis-interpretation of the lines from 'I am that E'. Nothing to do with the treatment of a newly emergent poet, but more to do with a marriage which altered in middle-age. If this isn't clear from the rest of the poem then it's a failure.

CR: You waited a long time to publish a first volume. Could you say more about this.

EB: I've always felt very ambivalent about publication and erratic about sending poems out and it wasn't until Harry Chambers asked if he could do a book that I agreed. I don't think I was so much a neglected poet as neglectful of the kinds of ways to get published at all. I'd seen enough of the rejections and very few acceptances of my husband's work over a number of years and his final giving up of writing to alert me to the anguish of not being wanted. It suited me to write without an audience so that I could do what I wanted without an editor or publisher. There were certain places where I knew I'd be welcome and two or three poems a year in print seemed fine. When *A Lifetime of Dying* first came out I cried a lot and wondered how I could burn all the books until a few reviewers responded favourably, which I never expected.

CR: I'd like to ask about your consciousness of being a 'woman poet'. Was this an issue for you early on, or were you relatively unconscious of the conflicts that might be inherent in being female and a writer?

EB: Such difficult questions! You're probably right to say that I was relatively unconscious of the conflicts that might be inherent in being female and a writer. I was more concerned with the act of writing itself and solving those problems of form and content which all poets have. In fact I was both secretive about writing and isolated from the literary world.

CR: Was the Women's Movement important to you, and if so, in what ways?

EB: In any real sense, no, it wasn't. When even I realized it was happening I suppose I felt it was not before time. I'm very bad at knowing about things in the outside world, living an intense inner life as I do, until perhaps I started to work in the Home Care service, and as a doctor's receptionist. This jolted me into writing about other people and thinking about an all too real world.

CR: What is the woman poet's symbolic relation to her poems? Are they her children, as you imply in 'Stretch Marks'? Why does she need symbolic as well as real children, if so?

EB: This tangled question of male creativity and poems as children made a kind of joke poem emerge for me ('Stretch Marks'), but only because at the time I seemed to be listening to a lot of male poets who were more than dominant at poetry readings. I still find most men pretty offensive in their attitudes to women, but at seventy it doesn't bother me so much. I don't know the answer to the symbolic relation of a woman poet to her poems. As you might have guessed by now, I don't seem to think on these lines. A real child is a physical thing, needing more care, love and attention than any poems will ever get. It's probably the hardest work any woman will do, but suddenly, they're away at school and there's time to write, to be oneself. Back to the scribbling and the private art!

CR: *Is there anything in the idea that there are special problems, intellectually, for women shifting from their traditional role as 'muse', to producer of literature? Perhaps there are advantages, too? Any comments? Were you ever a 'muse' and was this detrimental/empowering?*

EB: This question about women shifting from their traditional role of muse was/is no problem for women novelists. I'd much rather have been a novelist anyway, able to move between fact and fiction, which is still suspect in poetry. I do it all the time, but so far nobody has chided me for this. I was once my husband's muse in several stories, mostly young and rather dopey as indeed I was, but I only recognized this later. I used to get cross about this, which was ridiculous, I now see. He taught me a lot.

CR: *You wrote of Sylvia Plath: 'I tread her paths, but warily; avoiding the place/she finally found her deepest silence, her eternal bell-jar'. Despite this 'wariness' I felt that, in a few poems, Plath was an exemplar – eg 'The child is Charlotte'. However, it turns out that you wrote this poem in 1952, well before Plath was published in England. Any comments?*

EB: I don't accept this 'Plath as an exemplar' thing. What I do accept is that she was probably a depressive and I latch on to what I call the neurotic voice. We've covered this ground before. It has to do with intensity of feeling and mood swings so that the language becomes infused with this. One might be surprised how many poet's work springs from a similar source or episode.

CR: *Do you agree that a woman poet has a particular obligation to descend, like Persephone, to a very dark area of the self in order to emerge fully-fledged? Is this because women still feel seduced by the 'Angel in the House'? How compatible (for example) is being a poet with being wife and mother?*

EB: I'm not into Greek mythology, but as I remember, Pluto took Persephone to the underworld, captured her, indeed. Actually, she was the Roman counterpart I think. 'The Angel in the House' sounds like Coventry Patmore, but I'll stick with how compatible is being a poet with being a wife and mother. I've never found this difficult, except perhaps for those few months with a new-born baby. The making of a poem mostly goes on in the head anyway which can be combined with being an angel in the house, if that is what you call the basic kind of house-keeping and child-rearing I go in for. Dark areas of the self is something I know a lot about, but not, as you suggest, as an obligation in order to emerge fully-fledged as a poet. I would have been very grateful not to have gone into the underworld but left alone to pick daffodils. Proserpina, you will remember was doing just this when Pluto so rudely interrupted her. Hence the asphodel etc, etc.

CR: *Is writing healing and redemptive, or does it sensitize and produce a kind of 'vicious circle' of anguish?*

EB: Yes, both healing and redemptive often, but occasionally what you call a 'vicious circle of anguish'. This vicious circle of anguish is sometimes prolonged over several poems on one theme and eventually some of these have to be discarded. Tom Paulin in the *Observer* (5/6/94), when asked what writing poetry gives him, said: 'The most intense kind of happiness'. It's so rare that something would come into your head, you get a notion. You can't stop, it's like a physical hunger, you have to keep coming back to it, until you've finished or abandoned it'. Sometimes abandoning a poem makes the next one better. I'd agree with Paulin on this.

CR: *You have experienced horrors – those undramatic horrors of illness, poverty, death – which might have silenced you. How did you manage to cope, and to turn them into poetry?*

EB: Everyone, I think, has experienced horrors. I wouldn't call poverty a horror actually. My mother demonstrated to me the courage of working-class women, miraculously providing clean clothes, good meals, managing with minuscule amounts of money, loving, caring and worn out long before their time. Perhaps then, for me, writing was a way of coping. Being silenced, of course, means giving up, in a way. Nothing, so far, has silenced me for very long, which some critics might regret.

CR: *There seems to be a profound atheism underlying your work. For example, in 'Corpus Christi' there seems to be a bitter sense that God's mercy does not measure up to human suffering. Is this a fair comment?*

EB: I don't find it easy to comment on religion, although I wanted to be a believer as a child, because for the women in our household it was such a comfort. I incline more to the Buddhist view of life, without actually being one, and I practise meditation regularly. The scale of human suffering is so immense I cannot accept the idea of God as merciful and loving. Agnosticism rather than Atheism.

***CR:** You have a fascination with the misuse of language, e.g. Takao's question in 'A Translation': 'Do you remind of it?' Is the idea that poetry should push language to extremes, and offend conventions, a part of this fascination?*

EB: Well, playing around with words is great fun. There has to be some fun in this welter of words. All exciting art breaks the rules and pushes language to extremes, or in vision or music shakes it around a bit. Conventions do ask to be offended against.

***CR:** Have you ever done translation? What are your views on it in general?*

EB: No, no translating. I'm not good enough at foreign languages and I'm finding learning German now fiendishly hard. I always suspect a good translator makes another poem and a bad one diligently reduces it in some way.

***CR:** Can poetry entirely avoid élitism?*

EB: Not really, probably. What I consider to be fairly accessible and lucid poetry foxes most ordinary readers, I think. 'Modern poetry is so difficult' is what I hear all the time. Betjeman appeals to thousands, and few are aware of the sub-text even in this popular Poet Laureate.

***CR:** Painting and the visual arts: have these been an important inspiration?*

EB: Paintings are an important part of life for me. I enjoyed doing a poem about one of Gwen John's paintings in *With a Poet's Eye* – the Tate Gallery anthology, but they don't crop up as inspiration very often.

***CR:** Who is your ideal reader? What is your sense of your actual readership?*

EB: My ideal readers would have a knowledge of the unconscious and its workings, not be too fond of Keats, say, or Wordsworth, and not be too fearful of entering strange territories, states of mind or areas of life most poets avoid. They would be politically left of centre, not too respectable, and willing to buy copies of my collections for their friends and relations as well as themselves.

In sharp contrast, my actual readers are a Professor of English at an American university, his students, a student in Manila, a librarian in Canada, a writer in Cambridge, a Tory ex-Minister, and a lonely man in Germany who swears he wants to leave his 'considerable fortune' for my 'important litarec (sic) work'. Fellow poets of course, though we often have a swap system. Whoever bought all the rest is a mystery to me. Some get sold at readings which seems fair enough, as they've sampled the goods, so to speak.

***CR:** You are in your seventh decade, and you are writing as prolifically as ever. Do you feel that certain periods of your life have been creatively richer than others – if so, why?*

EB: True I hit the big seven-0 a few weeks back and could no longer say that I was in my late sixties any more and yes, perhaps I write too much. Certain periods of my life have been more creatively rich than others. During the five years of psychoanalysis in my late twenties, I wrote almost compulsively and there was so much material I hardly knew how to keep up with it. There was another body of work when I started working in the Home Care Service and as receptionist to a local doctor. Although in these two periods there was a lot of stimulation, I haven't found the quieter times any less productive. Sometimes one goes right back to a theme from another decade. I recently wrote a poem called 'Entering Language' (published in *The Forward Anthology 1993)* about my son's first words. It had taken me thirty eight years to view him from a different angle. In fact, it was so vivid I had to write it in the present tense, and it might well have been thought to be a young woman's poem.

***CR:** To rhyme or not to rhyme – is that a conscious decision each time you write?*

EB: Sometimes. I like all the problems rhymes present and overcoming them so that the seams don't show. I admire people like John Whitworth who do it most of the time, but I'm inclined to agree with my friend U. A. Fanthorpe that it's a bit like wearing a corset. Is it too naive to say that each poem demands what it needs? There's a particular moment when one has an image of the poems to come, like a pattern in the mind as if already laid out in stanzas or not, with or without rhymes, long and thin, or even flowing down the page like water. It's very mysterious really.

***CR:** You seem attracted by formality, but you rarely write actual forms from the literary tradition (sonnet, etc). Why is this? Was writing in strict form part of your apprenticeship?*

EB: Literary tradition was very much a part of a group of poets I used to belong to, headed by Laurence Lerner, in Brighton. We 'did' the sestina, the sonnet, the ballad, set subjects, the lot, and then we read them to each other and advised each other on what should be left in and what should be left out. It bloody nearly killed me. Three very good poets came from that group: Philip Gross, Nicky Rice and Laurence Lerner, but when I sometimes dream I'm back there, I wake up sweating.

***CR:** There seems to be a kind of push-pull dynamic between looseness and informality, and a more metrical tightness, in your technique. You are particulary successful in avoiding the tyranny of iambic pentameter,* *but you keep within 'talking distance' of it. Any comments?*

EB: I'd agree with you over what you call the push-pull dynamic between looseness and informality and a more metrical tightness in what you are kind enough to call my technique. This is the outcome maybe of all these problems we've been discussing. The good old tyrannical iambic pentameter is very useful and I shall continue, no doubt, to keep within talking distance of it. After all, for most of us, techniques are hard come by, whatever they are, and if they offend some people, we hope to write in our own way.

CR: You seem to me in some ways a poet who works by ear. Do you say your poems aloud as part of the process of composition and lineation?

EB: Working by ear is part of the process. The terrifying thing about writing poems is that sometimes you don't know what's going to happen, what emotions are going to be tapped, how you are going to deal with certain themes. A tape recorder is useful because it picks up hesitations in speech.

CR: How has the role of the poet changed in your lifetime?

EB: There are more poetry readings. Poetry itself is more accessible and as a lady said to me the other day, 'You're much too sensible and practical to be a poet'. This opening out into all aspects of life is very invigorating. We are now probation officers, even, or home helps.

ELIZABETH BARTLETT

Life Sentence

'It often happens that dreams manifest an extraordinary power of maintaining themselves in memory.'

The judge and jury assembled in the hours
between two and dawn, looming over the bed
where the prisoner turned and woke and feared
they could condemn her and cut off her head.

She thought the crime was infanticide or murder,
but, dazed by clips of film, muddle and confusion
surrounded everything. She picked up broken toys
and ran from her tormentors, confessed to collusion

with some partner, who was wearing the wrong face
over his old school tie and frowning slightly
as he gave his evidence that she was really
Lady MacBeth and not to be taken lightly.

Diligently scrubbing at her palm, she saw crowds
muttering in corners, but denied that she was ill
in any way or suffered from delusions of reference
or beamed on to rays which could slowly kill.

They changed the charges frequently to evade
the themes of disappointment, guilt and shame,
and bribed witnesses to affirm that she had
substituted fake stances, using another name.

And so she woke, and found it was only a dream,
as all good children's stories end to explain
why toys come to life from boxes and baskets,
but the sentence was one of life and endless pain.

Stepping into down-trodden slippers she felt
that the dream would stay with her all day.
The courtroom shadowed every door and corner
like a double exposure which would not go away.

SOPHIE HANNAH

In the Bone Densitometry Room

I could say that my life is my own
When you ask where I've been and with whom
But my voice has the tone
Of a powdery bone
In the bone densitometry room.

I could say there are rats in my throne,
I'm a helium bride with no groom,
Just a motorway cone,
And I crush like a bone
In the bone densitometry room.

It is not what you seek to postpone.
It is not what you wrongly assume.
This erogenous zone
Is as smooth as a bone
In the bone densitometry room.

Are my feelings as commonly known
As a raid on a high-rise in Hulme?
Are they tapping my phone?
Am I really a bone
In the bone densitometry room?

If my cover's already been blown
They can sweep me away with a broom.
When you leave me alone
I'm a shivering bone
In the bone densitometry room.

New Girl on the Block

Sophie Hannah was* Poetry Review*'s youngest ever New Poet in our 'Jostling at the Sacred Gates' issue in 1992. John Whitworth salutes her first collection:

Sophie Hannah,
The Hero and the Girl Next Door,
Carcanet, £6.95
ISBN 1 85754 113 8

While I am cleaning yoghurt from the crevices of my daughters' lunch boxes I listen to *Kaleidoscope* on Radio 4. *Kaleidoscope* is about the Arts and so presenters have that mixture of flip fatuity and youth which gives them street cred. Every now and again they yank in some nice Po-world guru to recite mantras about Poetry Now being Poetry Now and At The Cutting Edge and Relevant. The guru I am listening to is Maura Dooley, who is politer to them than they deserve.

Presumably Sophie Hannah will be getting the treatment and they will play variations on the theme of woman + gritty northern-ness + youth + rhyme 'n metre. And the other theme about whether poetry can be funny like the Luton bard or like (I shall scream) Wendy Cope.

Every time Sophie Hannah comes up we get stuff about the great Wendy Cope (whom God preserve). Is she a young, gritty northern Wendy? Is she better? Is she not as good? Whither the School of Cope? Arts-persons have all sorts of substitutes for thought. To say one writer/artist, whatever is like another is a good one. Are you an Irish poet? Then you're like Seamus Heaney. Are you from Hull? Philip Larkin. Huddersfield? Simon Armitage. Of course you can be not-like them. The important thing is you're docketed, nailed. Chris Reid has suffered from this – being the Second Martian is no job for a grown man but that's the way it goes. Someone asked me once which poet had most influenced me and I answered, truthfully, that it was Shakespeare. Would that be Fred Shakespeare from Barnsley?

I first met Sophie Hannah after a reading in Manchester. I second met Sophie Hannah on a Tŷ Newydd course. I was supposed to be teaching her. Can you imagine? One of our wheezes (this was Simon Rae's actually) was to get the apprentice poets to write a verse inspired by the day's newspapers (the *Sun* is good for this). Sophie retired to the *Sun*-drenched garden and returned with the one about fat girls containing this felicitous quatrain:

> You have to shed the pounds. It's such a drag.
> You can't rely on brains or sense of humour.
> It isn't true that many men will shag
> Virtually anyone – that's just a rumour.

(Though isn't the phrase 'virtually anything'?) Perhaps she'd written it already and was cheating. Or perhaps her poems do come to her with a Tommy Copper just-like-thatness. Can they be any good if you can do them so quickly? This was what mad Ruskin asked Whistler who told him that artists are not paid piece-work but for a lifetime's experience. But Sophie Hannah hasn't had a lifetime's experience. No – she's just a genius. What? You heard what I said. Shall I put it in capitals? SOPHIE HANNAH IS A GENIUS. Like Beethoven you mean. No. Like Rossini. And I bet she doesn't know how she does it. I hope she doesn't even think about it.

We're on the Light Verse thing now, aren't we? You can't win competitions with funny poems. Is Light Verse poetry? Are cartoons Art? Is the overture to *The Thieving Magpie* great music? Or Fats Waller singing *Ain't Misbehaving*. Do you like Beryl Cooke or Conceptual Dead Sheep? Great Comic Novels are allowed but what about Great Comic Poems? If *The Pickwick Papers* is good like *Wuthering Heights* is 'The Walrus And The Carpenter' good like 'The Waste Land'? Perhaps we can squeeze in Carroll because of the little girls with nothing on. Wound and Bow – poets are all mad. What about 'A Policeman's Lot' from the *Pirates Of Penzance*. Was Gilbert mad?

Sophie Hannah's book. OK. Not all the poems here are winners (though there's a high success rate). Some of them misfire. Some have faults of phrasing, even, to my ear, of rhythm. She will do better books and you can buy them when she does. Meanwhile get this one. If you are the right sort of person you will read it and laugh and read it again till it falls apart. It ought to win prizes but, being funny, it probably won't.

The high spirits have so infected Carcanet that they have given her a decent cover in place of the boring old rubbish they usually put round their poets. Covers are improving. Even Faber have done something about the horrible wallpaper they used – like junked it and not before time. Who does the best covers? Peterloo by miles. And Bloodaxe aren't bad. PUBLISHERS – DON'T SKIMP ON THEM. The cover is the first poem in the book. Unfortunately many poets are visually illiterate or they settle for what they can get. Or the publishers think they are in church and boringness is good for the soul.

I know that Sophie Hannah recently spent a year learning to write novels. So perhaps she won't stick at poetry. Her rate of writing is phenomenal, which is another of those things that make her unrespectable. Eliot, Larkin, Fenton – paucity is in. By the way, if we're playing the likeness game, she's like the Fenton of 'Wild Life Studies', very good Fenton for my money.

Some of the poems are quite odd. Try the beginning of this

> Fish Tony's Chips. The marble god has eyes.
> His handshake is a cupboard on the wall
> In which a cabbage rots and changes size.

Or the middle of this one.

> From time to time she'd blink and shout
> There's nothing to be dead about.

Or the whole of the sonnet 'The Shallow End'. This is the third quatrain:

> My ornaments were sad to see me go.
> I must remind them that we still vote Labour.
> Return the plum tomato that you owe.
> *I would like a hole in the garden to bury my neighbour.*

It reminds me of Carroll of course. And of Christian Morgenstern translated R.F. C. Hull. 'There was a sandwich paper which/Mysteriously began to itch'.

I last met Sophie Hannah judging the Canterbury Festival Poetry Competition. A 12-year-old won second prize in her section for a School-of-Hannah poem called 'I Dumped Him'. ('He was very spotty/The amount he ate alone drove me potty'.) They're turning up already. In a few years we'll be overrun. Remember, you heard it here first.

JAMES BERRY
Millennium Eyes

We could never see enough.
We gleaned only a little of what is.
A hidden past little understood
a future view still out of sight
we could never engage with a full account.

Nothing outside was believable
as the image seen. Delivered words
carried omissions and additions
and stayed with closed faces
when seeing exactly was crucial.

And we yearned. We yearned to see
to the bottom of reasons,
through walls and over horizons.
We needed others to absorb that violence
in the seared flesh of our pain
and see our needs
and their rooted establishments –
see all of a situation,
all of an outcome
with all its angles, way back to source.

Now astrology tells us
the millennium brings new eyes:
make eyes, wear them openly,

you grow more and more eyes inwardly.
And colleges start up eyemaking courses –
a craze with students everywhere now.

In shades of grey, green and diamond,
brown, orange, blue, black and purple,
worn as pendants or bracelets
or as a band around the head,
eyes are the latest adornments.

Couples newly wed stare into
each other's manufactured eyes:
people say they see their future in them.
And crowned, bangled, garlanded, hung
with eyes, student groups go about singing
'More eyes, more eyes, more eyes!
The millennium brings new eyes'.

James Berry's new collection,* Hot Earth, Cold Earth, *will be published by Bloodaxe in June.

KATE CLANCHY

Mitigation

We think you know the secret places,
the ones you called, perhaps, *Big Sands,*
The Den, or *Grassy Hill.* They loom up large
behind your eyes. Those hands that stroke
your signet ring were once, like ours, blunt-
fingered, small, and clutched at grass or clenched
a stone, and loved the tender, ticking throat

of panicked bird or retching child. You
watched the films, played Dracula,
That doll was yours whose head came off.
You stored her up behind the fort, the patch
of dirt around her mouth. There's something
buried in the park, a shallow grave, a rotting
thrush. You know the place. And know

the swooping railway tracks and why
we stole a child like humbugs from the shops.
You twitch and feel the small wet thrill.
You balked, you bottled, ran, that's all.
We heard you from the Policeman's van:
We heard your hands, the short, sharp slaps
of grown-ups clamouring to get back.

Kate Clanchy was born in Glasgow in 1965. She won a Gregory Award in 1994. Her first collection,* Slattern, *will be published by Chatto & Windus in the Autumn.

LAWRENCE SAIL
The Landscape of Threat

The end of surprise: or the start
Of an understatement that plays
The lower cases to advantage.
A matter of the ice, perhaps,
In the wind that swoops up to the ridge;
Or the water too cloudy to fathom
In the old ironstone quarries;
Or the light that sears like pure acid
At the rim of the rolling cloudbase.

Lost among fields, beyond
The saplings collared in tubes,
The works are long low buildings
Apparently deserted and closed.
But all of them, you are sure,
Have no end of little rooms
With darkening stains on the walls,
Windows that ward off the glare,
An atmosphere stale with questions.

Incidentals will do here: no need
For emblems. The imagination
Is a hostage to market forces,
And truth is nothing but fact.
On the road, the splayed fruit-skin
Means nothing, even if it makes you
Think of your head split wide open
On the tarmac. So why is your heart
Racing, and something telling you to run?

Lawrence Sail's new collection,* Building into Air, *will be published by Bloodaxe in October.

ROGER CRAWFORD
Spring Comes to St. John's Gardens

(for Paul Dutch)

Farewell to the winter, the snow-swirled statues
The frosted pigeons and the shimmering lamps;
Now the old philanthropes
Flash from their frockcoats
Wing from their collars
Twirl their moustaches and furl up their gamps –
while, prone to the greensward,
Snug in the sunshine,
Drift the rabbinical, simmering tramps.

Stony-faced Goddesses
Burst from their bodices;
Hun-helmeted Valkyries
Descend from their eyries,
The harpies of summer.
They goose the young drummer
And eye Tommy Atkins, who's trouncing the Boer;
While prone to the greensward,
Snug in the sunshine,
The simmering tramps turn over and snore.

Spring, like a prisoner sprung
has arisen! Her
Children are grey, but still they are spring's;
Abortionists, rapists,
Contortionists, typists,
Accept the protection of helmets and wings!

Farewell to the winter! the marbled flowerbeds!
The splintered benches!
The wind-rattled cans and the aches and the cramps!
Now the old philanthropes
Yo-yo their fingers,
Point to the sun with its trillion-watt lamps! –
while, prone to the greensward,
Snug in the sunshine,
Drift the rabbinical, simmering tramps.

BERNARD O'DONOGHUE

What's the Time, Mr Wolf?

Glass, someone once told me, is a liquid
of such density that its sluggish
Downward seep takes centuries to work,
So medieval windows are thicker
At the bottom than the top. If I push

My index-finger up along the bridge
Of my nose, I smooth away the wrinkles
I recall erasing with the same
(But smaller) finger from my mother's forehead
Forty years back, spiriting her frown away.

Have you noticed when you stand erect,
Breathing in, how your chest-flesh has
A tendency to droop towards the floor,
More markedly with every year
That passes? It creeps for the earth,

Like a child in a race stealing more odds
While the starter's back is turned,
Or the Pardoner's old man, tapping
The ground with his stick and pleading
'Dear mother, let me in'.

Bernard O'Donoghue's new collection,* Gunpowder, *will be published by Chatto in the Autumn.

The Promise Clinic

Helen Dunmore on first collections

Katherine Pierpoint, *Truffle Beds*,
Faber, £6.99
ISBN 0 571 17360 8
Ann Sansom, *Romance*,
Bloodaxe, £6.95
ISBN 1 85224 285 X
Robert Saxton, *The Promise Clinic*,
Enitharmon, £5.99
ISBN 1 8701612 39 6
Maurice Riordan, *A Word from the Loki*,
Faber, £6.99
ISBN 0 571 17364 0

New voices are often not so very new. By the time they get a whole collection to themselves they may have been working themselves up from a mutter for years, going through the paces of workshop group, small magazine, pamphlet, Gregory award. With luck, they are gathering strength. Sometimes, they are just getting louder. Katherine Pierpoint doesn't seem to be the product of this laborious, semi-public apprenticeship. She's gone very quickly to her first full collection, *Truffle Beds*, and her voice is brimming over with confidence, freshness, newness. The voice is almost too big for the poems sometimes. It makes them uneven, almost overwhelming, as if she cannot always modulate as she needs to do. But the degree of raw talent she shows here is quite arresting. There is the obvious feel for language, the lyricism, the grasp of image and metaphor, but beyond this there is something much rarer: an ability to make thought glow with the immediacy of sensory experience. 'Going Swimmingly' for example, makes a lovely double-take of the physical fact that we are nearly all water:

> The blue-rinsed pool is full of rythmic, lone
> strokers.
> It drew us in from the edges as though it were
> blotter-dry and we were rushing liquid.

Yes, maybe that 'blue-rinsed' is redundant, starting one hare too many, an instance of the too-muchness that can cloud these poems, but the use of 'rushing' is quite exceptionally imaginative and to the point. D. H. Lawrence is an obvious influence in this collection, particularly on such poems as 'Goatfall' or 'Jake the Blind Dog'. Pierpoint's country childhood is not a fuzzy or romanticised memory. She knows about animals, estuaries, cuckoo-spit and horse-doctors, and she's right there making them come alive, in close-up, wholehearted detail.

> How far he can swing into the hedge for buds
> too high for the nannies,
> Dabbing at the bread-and-cheese of hawthorn
> With thin, warm lips on a raw steel beak.
>
> That head – how close the warm bone lies to
> the surface –
> like touching the rocking, topmost stone of a
> cairn which may fall.
> ('Goatfall')

Pierpoint's movement through free verse is rapid and sure-footed. Her pacing is good in poems such as 'This Dead Relationship', where the astringency of her colloquial tone perfectly suits the subject. She is a poet to enjoy now, and I think and hope she is one to watch.

Ann Sansom

Ann Sansom's *Romance* strikes a cooler note. These are experienced poems, laconic and anecdotal. Here is a poet who has served all kinds of apprenticeships, who knows her territory, and speaks from within it with authority. A Catholic childhood, love and separation, the earthiness and poignancy of children, women's almost wordless signallings to one another over the comic awfulness of marriage ... her deliberately downbeat titles advertise a world where you may be chilled but you won't be fooled. 'Done With Mirrors', 'I'll Get Up Soon', 'Him Downstairs', 'Base Linguistics': the flatness of the titles is intelligently milked for the double-meanings of daily life:

> We are not girls. We weigh the things we're told
> and there is little that we swallow whole
> but sometimes there's a joke that makes you
> smile
> in the dark. It may be weeks before it makes
> you sick.

'Romance' is placed well towards the end of the book, riding on the back of all this salty realism. A grandfather tells his grandchildren his favourite tale of how he courted and won his wife 'the night at Gallagher's I played the flute'. He appeals to her for confirmation as she crosses the room with her arms full, headed for the kitchen. She smiles, and without breaking 'her long stride' flattens him with

> Indeed I do,
> And a terrible thing it was, if I may say so
> now.

The poem is complex. It's about anger and disappointment, yes, but it's also about a kind of romance where the woman guards herself over decades by withholding the easy assent that her husband only thinks he wants.

Ann Sansom is acute in her understanding of people who do not necessarily put their emotional sophistication into words. These poems look at what language can't do, as well as what it can. They explore the potential of a well-worn phrase to detonate when placed in a particular context. The short poem 'Felix 11' turns succinctly and memorably on the fact that a son unconsciously uses the polite formula of a visitor to express a shift in a relationship:

> *Mum. Dad said to call and say*
> *I landed home all right ...*
> you hesitate, worried,
> *Oh, yes. And thank you for having me.*

It's a very powerful moment, even though, unusually, Ann Sansom misjudges the point at which she should end the poem, and adds another verse to it. Sansom's voice throughout the collection is admirably clear and honest. The poems do not make fools of themselves, and there are no excesses, fine or otherwise.

Robert Saxton

Robert Saxton certainly has his excesses in *The Promise Clinic*. He's pedalling on his unicycle, which is balancing on a ball held on the nose of a sea-lion which is ... But he doesn't fall off. It's nice to watch, though sometimes more difficult to enter into the poem and feel its sense as strongly as one feels the lovely, pointless charm of its artistry. Saxton loves form, and how he can stretch it to let in the words he wants, then snap it shut again. His sestina 'Esperanto Nights' orchestrates its repetitions so that they unsettle as surely as Auden's. No matter how bleak his material, he's having fun. It's instructive to compare his poem about climbing a steeple, 'Foraging' with Katherine Pierpoint's 'Steeplejack'. (And why is it that poems on certain subjects seem to arrive all at the same time bunched like buses?) Pierpoint is all sensuous connections, a river of language pouring upwards. Saxton is condensed and off-beat, and then suddenly he pulls off an almost deranged feat in his final simile. The scratching of twigs

> ... felt like my grandmother's
> Fingernails ambushing me
> In the one place I hadn't thought of.

The inside of Robert Saxton's mind seems not to be much like any other poet's, but he has sufficient élan to make readers see things his way, if only for the moment. 'The Manatee and the Dugong' opens with a flourishing simile and knocks its subject swiftly into shape with a combination of rhyme, adroit buttonholing on unlikely side-issues, and restless observation:

> Their backs all rutted from propeller blades,
> Crisscrossing scars half-voluntary like
> sunburn.

Of the poets here, Saxton and Riordan are perhaps the most systematically curious about language. The idea of Esperanto recurs in Saxton's poems, signifying non-communciation and specialised private language, as well as the dream of a common language. He emphasises the oddity of communication, and the boldness and pathos of our assumption that we understand one another when we speak.

Maurice Riordan

Maurice Riordan opens his first collection with a poem called 'Time Out' which tells a story of the type published in the *Guardian*'s Saturday supplement feature 'Urban Myths'. Yeah, it really happened, this friend of a friend of mine told me ... It's puzzling to know quite what 'Time Out' adds to the genre, unless in making a self-conscious step outside the narrative towards the end. Fortunately, Riordan is a better poet than his first poem suggests. The title poem, 'A Word from the Loki', makes effective play of its own pedantry, but it moves beyond this to a sadness which is almost classical in its purity. The same sadness, this time tinged with a distillation of anger, pervades 'The Check-up – June 1992'. Here

> God, coming back from his tour of the
> galaxies,
> decides to drop in on Earth.

The poem manages its central idea with warmth and humour, which again suddenly darkens at the end as God spots a detail

> something slight
> – but unprecedented, unforeseen – that wipes
> the smile
> clean from his face.

It's not that the idea is so very original, but the handling is so apt, tactful and well-pitched that it makes a notable poem. Riordan is in his early forties, and this is a mature collection both artistically and emotionally. He has a beguiling manner in the telling of anecdotes from his childhood in

County Cork, and while these poems do not often make that imaginative acceleration beyond the particular which a poet such a Muldoon seems to achieve without strain, they are very readable. His tactic seems to be to bathe the unremarkable in attention and to write poems on largely everyday subjects which possess their own propriety, humour and grace.

Helen Dunmore's new novel,* A Spell of Winter, *was published by Viking in March.

Poetry Season '95 - Highlights

APRIL

Ivan Lalic, *A Rusty Needle,* Anvil. More of Francis Jones's prize-winning translations of the great Serbian poet.

Poetry of the Second World War, ed Desmond Graham, Chatto. The first WWII anthology to include European as well as British and American poets.

Charles Simic, *Frightening Toys,* Faber. The Yugoslav/American poet will come into his own with this new collection.

Ian Duhig, *The Mersey Goldfish,* Bloodaxe. The second collection by the poet much admired by Neil Kinnock and Roy Hattersley.

Eavan Boland, *Object Lessons* (essays), Carcanet. Not many poets make major essayists. Boland looks set to make the transition.

Helen Vendler, *The Given and the Made* (essays), Faber. There is no equivalent to Vendler here – a controversial public intellectual whose territory is poetry.

MAY

Michael Longley, *The Ghost Orchid,* Cape. New collection from a Whitbread winner. Poems of great delicacy with a strong classical feel.

***Penguin Modern Poets* launch: 1) James Fenton/Kit Wright/Blake Morrison; 2) Carol Ann Duffy/Eavan Boland/Vicki Feaver; 3) Glyn Maxwell/Mick Imlah/Peter Reading.**

Margaret Atwood, *Morning in the Burned House,* Virago. Her first new book of poems for 10 years.

Naomi Wallace, *To Dance a Stony Field,* Peterloo. First collection by an American poet now living in England; Second Prize Winner in 1994 National Poetry Competition.

JUNE

James Lasdun, *The Revenant,* Cape. Long awaited second collection by the most darkly elegant of the younger poets.

Sean O'Brien, *The Deregulated Muse* (essays), Bloodaxe. O'Brien is currently the only poet-critic punching his weight in both departments.

Peter Reading, *Collected Poems 1: 1970-1984,* Bloodaxe. The only poet we can think of whose Collected Poems have required two volumes within his lifetime.

JULY

Czeslaw Milosz, *Facing the River,* Carcanet. Milosz's last book was one of his best so there are high expectations for this one.

The New French Poetry (ed David Kelly, Jean Khalfa), Bloodaxe. At last France gains parity with all the other European countries that have produced 'New Poetry's' in translation.

Modern Hungarian Poetry (ed Szirtes/Gomori), Bloodaxe. Szirtes is the best guide we have to Hungarian poetry.

Summer *Poetry Review* Europe. Our first European issue since the Cheltenham Festival issue in '91 ('invaluable' – Denis Healey). Seamus Heaney and Stanislaw Baranczak's translations of Kochanowsky's *Laments;* Miroslav Holub on the *Chatto Book of Word War II Poetry.*

SEPTEMBER

Ted Hughes, *Difficulties of a Bridegroom,* Faber. The Hughes books keep coming – this is his first new collection since Wolfwatching (1989).

Simon Armitage, *Dead Sea Poems,* Faber. Armitage almost manages a book a year – can he keep it up?

Seamus Heaney, *The Redress of Poetry,* Faber. Heaney's essays and lectures are almost as famous now as his poems. These are the fruits of his Oxford Professorship.

OCTOBER

12th: Forward Prize. Best Collection £10,000; Best First Collection £5000; Best Poem in a Magazine £1000. Judges: Carol Ann Duffy, Peter Forbes, Lord Gowrie, Alan Jenkins, William Sieghart.

Poetry Society: *Poetry Books for Christmas.* Poetry normally drops of the map in the Christmas book bang. Not this year. A New Generation-style promotion will highlight 40 books of every kind, including biographies, books for children and anthologies. 16 page booklet. This will be included with the autumn *Poetry Review*, which will highlight the reading of poetry. Also, the **European Poetry Translation Prize** (judges to be announced in next issue).

Carol Rumens, *Best China Sky,* Bloodaxe. Rumens has entered a new phase with her engagement with Ireland.

Strathspeys and Death Metal

Don Paterson on the big and the little musics in Ted Hughes

Ted Hughes,
New Selected Poems 1957-1994,
Faber, £14.99 hbk; £7.99 pbk
ISBN 0571 17378 0

Ah, the great levellers – toothache, death and the spellcheck. Strange how our essential natures seem to lie buried in our names, as if it were only a small matter of scraping away a little typographical encrustation to lay bare the personality beneath... *WB Yeast. TS Elite. Seems Heavy.* My own favourite, the Boston Confessionalist, *Robot Lonely.* Big Ted comes out variously as *Tweed Hunches, Toad Haggis* and *The Hague,* all of which fit the bill rather well. The computer's last stab hit the spot exactly, though – get this: *Dead Huge,* two of his very favourite epithets.

Reviewing Hughes is quite the worst way to read a poet so overwhelmingly intense, and often pessimistically so. Hoping Hughes will lighten up is like waiting for the jokes in Tolstoy; reading him at length feels like you've spent the entire day listening to late Schoenberg, who was all dominant and no tonic. It's also remarkable that such a frequently difficult poet should be so popular. The *Hawk in the Rain* and *Lupercal* have, though, been thoroughly misrepresented by anthologists: neither 'The Thought-Fox' nor 'Esther's Tomcat' are particularly typical of either book, and any teenager who encounters these poems on the school syllabus, then rushes out to buy the books is likely to return home deeply confused, if not disappointed.

The Hawk in the Rain is still a stunning debut, however, astonishingly free from detectable influence other than maybe late Auden; I suspect I'm only thinking *that* because Hughes exhibits the same tendency towards self-conscious over-embroidery, even if the whole, as in 'Egg-head' or 'Fallgrief's Girlfriend', is beautifully put together; occasionally though, there's a tendency for the main theme to get lost below its own dense elaboration, like a watch with so many tiny hands and sub-dials it actually becomes difficult to tell what the time is. The earlier 'animal' poems (hereafter referred to as the 'animal' poems), are extremely fine, though they do not penetrate the identity of his subjects to anything like the same depth as Les Murray's 'Presences', say; this is no criticism of the poems themselves – at a stage of Hughes' career when he often seemed determinedly unautobiographical, they are as much projections of Hughes' own personality as anything else. Stevens, I think, crops up a bit in ' A Man Seeking Experience Enquires His Way Of a Drop of Water', but this (reviewer's nightmare) is the last time Hughes sounds like anything under the sun. 'Meeting' is another stunner, but 'Six Young Men' makes explicit Hughes' talent for overstatement which will not be properly exorcised until *Crow.*

Lupercal is still my favourite Hughes book, though H. seems terrified that unless every poem is dragged into the universal context it will somehow lose impact; the words 'globe' or 'world' occur in thirteen out of the twenty-one poems included here, which is far too often. Despite this, 'View of a Pig', 'Pike', 'November', and 'A Woman Unconscious' are still great poems. 'Pike' especially, as it contains an anecdote, another thing you tend not to get much of with Hughes. Again, that's only a neutral observation, but I still find it strange that Hughes, a wonderful storyteller, has almost totally eschewed narrative in his adult work. The few exceptions, such as the tragic birth of the lamb described in *Moortown Diaries,* could hardly have been told more vividly or movingly. Already, though, one can sense Hughes becoming impatient with those poetic conventions – consistency of metaphor, location, etc. that allow the reader to 'make sense' of the poem; 'making sense' becomes less and less of a priority, as Hughes' poems become more improvisatory, patterns of energy and association that the reader is required to meditate upon like a mandala.

Wodwo goes further out on a limb than ever; it is a cold, fascinating, thoroughly encoded book. One is perhaps too keen to praise poems like 'The Warriors of the North' and 'Out' for their comprehensibility alone. In *Wodwo* Hughes, you feel, is deliberately flinging the paddle overboard and cheerfully heading for the shit creek of *Crow.* He takes less and less pleasure in detail – wherein we all know God resides – as he is drawn towards the altogether godless imaginative territory he will occupy for some time. The 'animal' poems, are less effective here; his *constantly* imputing an absence of morality to them – in the very way he first indulges then recoils from it – strikes me as a kind of inverted sentimentalism.

'God screamed / And the whole earth / Contracted around its centre / Crow's dead pupil / Twitching, anguished...' That's from 'Crow's Contact Lenses'. No it's not. I just made it up. It isn't as good as Ted's stuff, but it *nearly* is, which is worrying. Now is the time, I suppose, to come forward and say that I do not think *Crow* is any good. At least it allowed Hughes to attribute all the nasty, selfish, brutal qualities he liked to one wee bird without calumniating the rest of the Animal Kingdom. There's a line at the end of 'Lineage', 'trembling featherless elbows in the nest's filth', which has always struck me as a good example of Hughes' peculiar and wonderful anti-music – a line you almost have to spit out; but there's almost nothing of Hughes' own characteristic, *inimitable* voice here. This is entirely deliberate, but the wilful suppression of technique means there's hardly a good line in *Crow*. James Kelman's 'notorious' overuse of the word 'fuck' nullifies the effect of it entirely, which is just the point of the exercise; Hughes uses the words 'death' and 'black' with the same profligacy, but still, one assumes, expects them to strike the reader with the same force. *Crow* is the Death Metal of poetry, a piece of hysterically sustained mythopoeia which has consciously sacrificed music for effect, and in doing so – since music is the only way in which poetic effect can be embodied – has no effect whatsoever, unless you can buy into it at the same pitch of hysteria; hence its continued popularity amongst adolescents and the mentally disturbed.

Chronologically in the middle of all this, we get the very wonderful and uncollected 'You Hated Spain', knocked off the way Picasso used to knock of the odd brilliant naturalistic portrait at a stage of his career when he was trying to paint like a five-year-old with the attention span of a goldfish. The poem tells of the Hughes' trip to Spain, and is somewhat at variance with the account of it given in Sylvia's letters. It's a beautiful poem by a consummate master, which I'd happily swap for all of 'Crow':

> ...I see you, in moonlight
> Walking the empty wharf at Alicante
> Like a soul waiting for the ferry,
> A new soul, still not understanding,
> Thinking it is still your honeymoon
> In the happy world, with your whole life
> waiting,
> Happy, and all your poems still to be found.

And it is with some relief that we turn to *Season Songs*, 'for children', it says here; it isn't, really – it just plays as a U certificate to *Crow*'s 18, so it must have seemed to Hughes like kids' stuff at the time. It's full of delightful things, though; 'Sheep' is quite breathtaking, as moving as the best of Frost; Hughes' wonderfully humane and human response to the plight of the deformed lamb is so skilfully communicated that only the reader with a heart of stone could fail to weep. Of that widely-remaindered turkey, *Rain Charm for the Duchy*, the less said the better. That a man of such singular intelligence – by whatever recondite agenda – could write a prothalamium for those monstrous twerps Fergie and Andy ('A helicopter snatched you up. / The pilot, it was me') and regard the result with anything other than abject embarrassment is a profound mystery to me.

What is the Truth? is another kid's book, and a lot of fun; although Hughes' attempts to jauntify his favourite themes are highly amusing: 'After that comes Orf – known as Lewer./ Ulcers of the nose, of the lips, of the eyes, of the toes... Awful things waiting for lambs ... Just trotting about gives him footrot. That is, his hooves fall apart / Exactly like rotten mussels...' ('The Problem about Lambs'). Mummy, I don't want Uncle Ted to read us to sleep again.

I don't think Hughes has written at full strength since *Flowers and Insects* – 'In The Likeness of a Grasshopper' is a beautiful poem – but the new work at the back of the book has a generosity and openness I don't think we've seen in Hughes before; for that reason, there's also plenty of meat for the vultures to fight over, which is why I'm not going to quote. Check it out.

Up here, bagpipe music is divided into the *Ceol Mor* and the *Ceol Beag*, the big music and the little music. The big music is the *pibroch*, the laments that you play on the battlements or in the great halls, those interminable threnodies with their thirteen classical variations. No-one pretends to like it anymore. You were never supposed to like it in the first place; it was about enforcing solemnity. The *ceol beag* is the jigs, reels, strathspeys, airs; the detail, in other words, the human detail, the little joys and griefs and loves. Hughes was a court bard even before his official investiture, and has always made the appropriate racket for the larger acoustic. He will come into his own when the House of Windsor (soon, it is to be hoped) start chucking a few snuffers. But Hughes' little music is so fine, and quite inimitable; it's a shame he doesn't enjoy it as much as we do.

There is one story and one story only, as your man said, but it is longer than the way Hughes tells it. Nonetheless, he has written his chapter with tremendous energy and vivacity, even if his bit is usually freeze-framed as the sky darkens over Golgotha, or the suitors lie dead at the feet of Odysseus. Perhaps he has been sensible in his specialisation. While the rest of us boys and girls sit swapping tunes round the hearth, maybe there should always be one man on the battlements, practising for Doomsday, for the time when the rest of us will be stuck for words, and for a song.

Electric Avenues

Leon Cych on a new resource for poetry: the Internet

About a year ago I started to research the Internet and the poetry resources on it in depth. Because I help edit a poetry networking magazine, I immediately saw the potential of this new medium for extending the boundaries of disseminating poetry resources and listings information throughout the English speaking world. I began my research by reading several specialist books on the subject and each left me with exactly the same feeling: that I was wading ever deeper into a steeply inclined morass filled to the brim with treacle. Before I knew it, I was drowning in a self-induced (and very sticky) cud of acronyms and jargon. Take this paragraph for instance:

> So you want to Cybersurf on the Infobahn. No need any longer to be an anorak, geek or nerd, just logon to the PoP at your local Service Provider, download their software then FTP to get a copy of your favourite browser. This'll let you post an email to Usenet but be sure to observe the right netiquette or you might get flamed. Try GOPHERING to JUGHEAD or VERONICA and picking up all those invaluable freeware applications. Then surf those amazing World Wide Web pages by clicking on hypertext, typing in the URLs or looking them up on your hotlist.

(If you can understand all this then you don't need to read this article!)

I don't know about you but IMHO (sorry – it's catching – In My Humble Opinion) this kind of thing leaves me more than a little bemused and it can drive some people to dementia even before they get near a computer. I read the books and read them again and thought I had an inkling – but I was wrong! In the intervening months things have got a little easier and I'm fairly confident I now know what I'm doing (and talking about) and that the process of getting onto the Internet is a little less arduous than learning Sanskrit.

So what is the Internet, what do you need to get onto it and what poetry resources are out there?

The Internet is twenty-five years old and is simply a system of computer networks connected together. It was established by the US military at the height of the Cold War to render their communications system impervious to nuclear attack – if one computer network was destroyed then information would be rerouted via another; it has been religiously subverted by the academic community for its own purposes ever since. In those intervening years many universities and educational establishments all over the world have built up huge information resources and databases. These massive databanks constitute a world library containing information on almost any subject that you can think of. During the last two years the Internet has been the subject of a lot of media hype because a scientist at CERN called Tim Berners-Lee wrote a program called Mosaic which made it possible for novice computer users to click on highlighted words, pictures or buttons in documents and locate data anywhere in the world instantaneously. The World Wide Web had arrived and many businesses and individuals have hooked up to take advantage of this 'new' medium for communication.

Most computers can now connect up to the Internet. Suitably fast equipment would be a 386, 486 or Pentium PC (a Dos operating system will do but Windows is better) or an AppleMac, a fast modem, a service provider and a phone line – I am not going into the mechanics of how to set these up in detail because there are too many variables involved and there are numerous books and magazines tailored to your particular system showing you how to do it.

A modem (or modulator demodulator – is that easier?) is a small box that fits between your computer and the phone line and enables you to dial in to a service provider. A service provider is an organisation that gives you access to the Internet and related services. If you are at University or work for a large business, then you are probably already connected. If not, then you will have to pay a service provider to get you online. This is usually about £10.00 a month + phone bills. If you don't live close to what is called a PoP, then you might have to pay more than the local-call phone rate. Your service provider should give you suitable software to get up and running. You will then need to connect up to them using a modem.

Connecting up the modem to your computer at one end and the phone line at the other and getting it to communicate with your service provider can be a little tricky – you may have to make several phone calls before the process all falls into place. I would recommend getting an experienced friend to help you if you have never done this sort of thing. Buy the fastest modem you can afford because the faster the modem the less time spent on the phone and the cheaper your phone bills.

Once you have connected everything to everything else and it works(?), then the first thing that you will encounter will almost certainly be email. Most service providers will give you an email address where you can be contacted, plus the software to enable you to send and receive mail in this way. For instance my email address is leonc@easynet.co.uk and my magazine's address is poetry@poetry.demon.co.uk – the Poetry Society's email address is poetrysoc@bbcnc.org.uk. The first part of these addresses is the unique user name, then comes the @ (at) symbol, followed by the name of the company, institution, university and then the domain name (the country or company). You can see by the above that the Poetry Society's service provider is the BBC Networking Club. There is a definite hierarchy in these addresses with the more prestigious ones being in the American military and educational institutions (they are the oldest).

Electronic mail enables you to send a letter anywhere in the world for the cost of a local phone call. Not only that, you can send as many letters as you want simultaneously for exactly the same cost. No wonder nearly every big business is connected by email. It is estimated that in the US, nearly 20% of traditional post has been lost to this system. The benefits of email are that it is fast – a message can travel round the world in as little as 20 seconds, and it is efficient – no paper, ink, stamps or transport costs. It is also very easy to archive all your posts as they come in, sorting them into different folders according to subject or person. Sending a letter back to someone who has emailed you is just a matter of typing some words into a program similar to a word-processor and clicking a couple of buttons. The downside is that it is all too easy to make a rash and ill-considered comment and post it off without thinking about how the person receiving the message will react. This happens all the time on the Internet and is considered bad Netiquette. It is always best to stop and think before sounding off and verbally blundering into conversation with other people by email. Some people use what are called 'Smileys' (sic); these are little typographic devices combining elements from the computer keyboard to display a picture like this **:-)** (a smiling face when seen on its side) – this denotes the use of irony for those people who are unable to master this written form. Emailers also often use irritating TLA's (three letter acronyms) such as BTW (by the way) TIA (thanks in advance) and ETLA's (extended three letter acronyms) such as ROTFL (rolls on the floor laughing). The style of an email letter tends to be a hybrid between conversation and postcardese: short, to-the-point statements often conveying information. A lot of emailers annotate the letters they have received from others replying point-for-point. In the course of writing this article I was in regular correspondence with academic institutions in the United States; each time all it cost was the price of a local phone call.

Poetry Society email:
poetrysoc@bbcnc.org.uk
Poetry London Newsletter
email:
poetry@poetry.demon.co.uk

With email it is possible to join one of the specialist 12,000 (and rising) usenet newsgroups and have electronic conferences with others connected to the net. A usenet newsgroup consists of a sort of electronic bulletin board of email posts from people all over the globe interested in a specific topic or hobby. The ones specifically related to poetry and literature are: rec.alt.poems which is abysmal but can be fun at times. This is filled with poems by poetry neophytes asking for constructive criticism and subsequent varied responses ranging from the outright abusive to the cringingly banal. Most useful criticism in this group consists of private email between individuals behind the scenes. The interesting postings on rec.alt.poems (rap for short) are announcements or requests, despite the fact that I must have seen 'What was that poem in *Four Weddings and a Funeral?'* posted countless times. Once you have this facility, try it out, post off a request for the source with a quote from your favourite poem – you are bound to get a reply within a few days. Better groups to read are rec.alt.books and rec.alt.books.reviews for their 'meatier' conversation and resources. I was able to post a review by Brian Docherty on Douglas Dunn's *Dante's Drumkit* and the Faber Scottish Poets on Burns night – this article was read by as many as 60,000 people worldwide. It generated a lot of supportive email correspondence, and one university wished to archive the text. It is also possible to have ezines (electronic magazines) posted to you automatically by email. Subscription is usually free but do you want that volume of mail on your hard disk each week?

The second most useful piece of software handed out by your service provider is a Web browser. This enables PC users with Windows software and AppleMac owners to view World Wide Web pages.

WWW pages usually contain pieces of information comprising graphics and text. What makes WWW pages so revolutionary is that they contain (take a deep breath) Hypertext. If you have used a CD-ROM encyclopaedia on a computer you will already recognise the concept of Hypertext. Certain words in the text that comes up on your browser software are a different colour (usually red or blue depending on your system) and are underlined. Click onto these words or letters with your mouse pointer and you are taken to a new, related document which could be held on another computer half way around the world. All WWW pages are held on computer servers around the world. A lot of information and WWW pages have been built up by maverick academics purely for their pleasure. All Web pages have an address called a (watch out, another TLA coming up) URL. A URL (Universal Resource Locator) is a way for the Web to specify where a particular resource is located on the Internet, but think of it simply as an electronic address. The best Web page browser is called Netscape (also known as Mozilla). It's what's known in the trade as a killer application and no, that does not mean poisonous suntan oil. My magazine *Poetry London Newsletter* has a Web page – anyone who types in the letters:

http://www-bprc.mps.ohio-state.edu/cgi-bin/hpp/poetry.html

into the URL box of their Web page browser will see our page flash up on their computer screen. Certain words and phrases are underlined. If you click onto those words with a mouse pointer, then you will be taken automatically to other poetry Web resources on the Internet. One of the best ones that I have come across is the Alderman Library's Hypertext archive at the University of Virginia at:

http://www.lib.virginia.edu/etext/britpo/britpo.html

If you look carefully at the above address you can work it out. Reading from right to left: britpo.html is the document containing the information about British Poetry 1780-1910, html stands for hypertext markup language, britpo is probably the directory on the computer server that this file is held in, etext is the directory that holds all the etexts (electonic texts) at the University of Virginia, www.lib.virginia.edu is the address of the Web page on the server at the Alderman library at the University of Virginia. This page is probably one of the best on the net at the moment but the British Library also has a wonderful Web site at:

http://service1.uky.edu/ArtsSciences/English/Beowulf/

I'll leave you to work that one out for yourself!

There are literally thousands of poetry resources out there all inextricably linked on the Web. Hence the terms Net and Web. Not surprisingly, there isn't much contemporary poetry and maybe this is a role for the Poetry Society in the future months. It certainly beats the hell out of two baked bean cans and roll of string!

JARGON BUSTING

***Anorak* – Completely derisory term for anyone who engages in excessive Cybersurfing and whose dress sense leaves a lot to be desired.**

CERN – The European Particle Physics Laboratory.

***Cybersurfing* – Hopping from resource to resource over the Internet. It also helps to have speed reading skills and the attention span of a flea.**

***Download* – Not what you might think! To get software, text, images etc from another computer via the phone line down to your computer's hard disk.**

***email* – An invaluable tool to communicate across the Internet or alternatively a piece of software that enables you to be spiteful, abusive and thoroughly annoying to people you've never met.**

***Flame* – Abusive email response to intentional/unintentional transgression of the unwritten codes of Internet etiquette or just pure vituperation for the sake of it!**

***Freeware* – Software that is free for the taking.**

FTP – File Transfer Protocol. Connecting your computer up to the Internet and then to a remote computer. Then passing files over to that computer or taking them from that distant computer's hard disk to your own.

GOPHER – A piece of software that 'goes for' (hmmm...) the piece of information you're looking for. A search and retrieval tool – so it brings it back. Type in the word POETRY into your GOPHER software search and see what happens!

***Hotlist* – A personal list kept on your browser software of your favourite Web pages.**

***Hypertext* – Text, that when 'clicked' on with a computer mouse links to another Web resource page. Very hard to define unless you've used it. *(Hence html* – hypertext markup language.)**

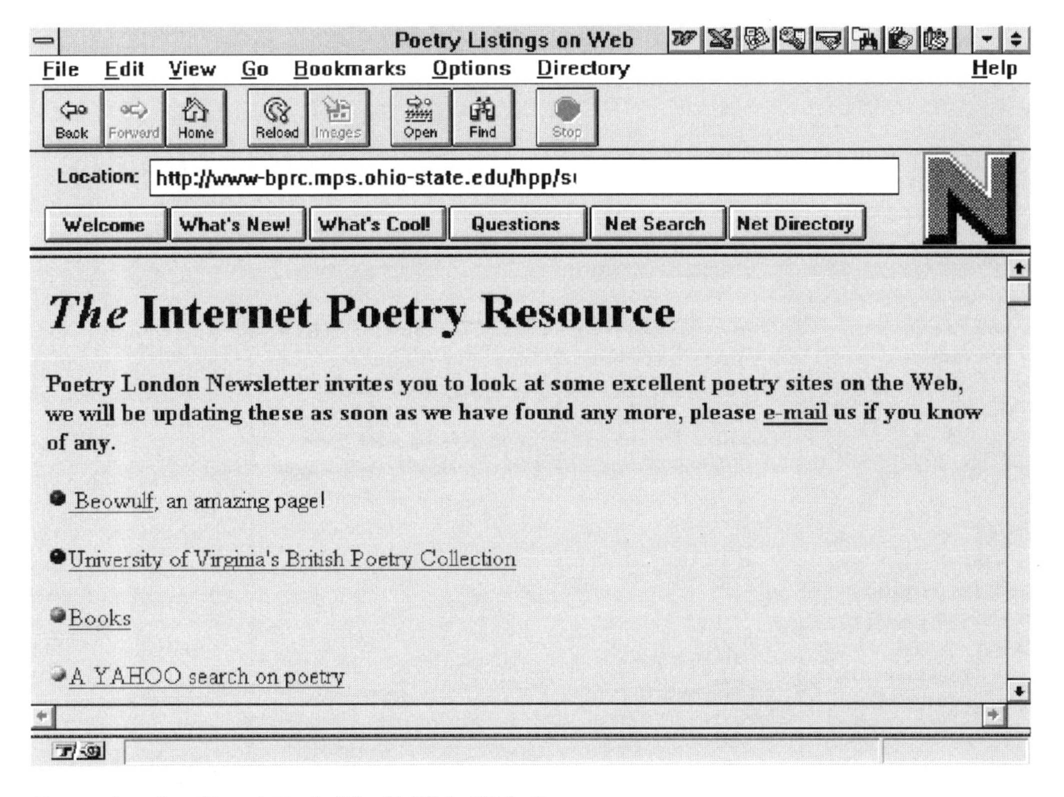

Poetry London Newsletter's World Wide Web Page

Infobahn – Silly made-up German name for the just as silly Information Superhighway.

JUGHEAD – Another search and retrieve tool acronymed spuriously after the Archie comic books of the 50's and 60's.

Logon – Turn on your computer and connect up to the Internet.

Service Provider – Someone who takes money off you in exchange for giving you access to the Internet.

Netiquette – Good manners on the Internet. Think before you make an outrageous or insulting comment in response to someone else's inflammatory remarks. Do not post advertisements for haemorrhoid cream to the usenet group UK.Singles for example.

PoP – Point of Presence. A connection point you can hook up to your service provider to make local phone calls onto the Internet. Alternatively what happens to your brain when the connection stops working.

URL – Universal Resource Locator. A way for the Web to specify where a particular resource is located on the Internet.

usenet – Over 12,000 special interest newsgroups on the Internet.

VERONICA – Acronym for Very Easy Rodent-Oriented Net-wide Index to Computerised Archives. This is goes out and performs a keyword search of all the Gopher-servers in the world. Again, type in POETRY and see what comes up.

BOOKS

The Whole Internet - User's Guide and Catalog, Ed Krol, O'Reilly and Associates, Inc. £18.50. This is probably the most authoritative book on the Internet but the speed of change has rendered it a little out-of-date on browsers etc. Still the best for how the Internet actually works.

The UK Internet Book, Sue Schofield, Addison Wesley, £19.9. A good read and funny too. Demystifies a lot of the jargon. Includes a free connection to Demon for one month.

Internet UK, Ivan Pope, Prentice Hall. £19.95. Clear, no-frills guide to the Internet with lots of info. Includes a free connection to Cityscape for one month.

World-Wide Web, Mosaic and More, Jason J Manger, McGraw-Hill, £25. One of the best books on the different Web browsers, how to write home Web pages.

SOME MAGAZINES

When it comes to up-to-date information about the Net, books are a little slow as a medium; magazines are a far better and cheaper way of finding out about the best current information resources out there. Just a few of the recent releases are:

Internet – The Practical Guide to What's On and Where to Go, emap business communications – One of the less hype-ridden publications for the more sober/ business user, it has less pretty pictures and more information. £1.50.

Internet World, Meckler-media Corporation – Good solid American magazine with lots of information. £2.95

.net, Future publications – Very glossy – themed issues, e.g the Net and virtual love, the Net and rock 'n' roll etc. £2.95. They are bringing out some very cheap *.net* guides see the mag for details.

Internet and Comms today, Paragon publishing – not as flashy as *.net* but still aimed at a youth market. Plenty of graphics and bylines. £2.95.

Wired – The most stylish magazine about the Web, but covers Technology in general. An American mag but a British version (good – just look at the price!) in a deal with the *Guardian* due out soon. £3.75.

POETRY SOCIETY DIRECTOR, CHRIS MEADE, WRITES: *Because the Internet relies on the power of the written word, because it turns your solitary computer screen into the entrance to a massive virtual library and writers' workshop of the world, because it helps us meet our two priorities: 1) to play a key, strategic role as a national organisation and 2) to maximise the benefits of our central London headquarters... and because there is an urgent need for poets to inject some form, content and brevity into the jargon-strewn depths of cyberspace, the Poetry Society has gone on-line.*

We've already started work on The Poetry Map in collaboration with the BBC Networking Club and the UK Year of Literature & Writing. The map will be available later this year on the World Wide Web. As well as information about the funding, publishing and performance of poetry, the map will also include specially commissioned new work and lively discussion about what helps poetry thrive.

By the end of this year we intend to have opened up the ground floor of Betterton Street as a new kind of Poetry Place: an information and imagination centre for poetry where members and the general public can savour good coffee, cakes and poetry, have access to the Poetry Map and other Internet services, word-processing and desktop publishing, books and magazines, information and exhibitions. We'll be running training workshops for poets, librarians, teachers and other groups as well as readings and launches. The place will be a stimulating and enjoyable public face for the service we provide to all our members nationwide via publications, phone... and now computer console.

SERVICE PROVIDERS – The people who get you up and running!

BBC Networking Club – Registration £25 and £12 a month. PO Box 7, Broadcasting Support Services, London W3 6XY. Phone: 0181 576 7799. Fax: 0181 993 6281. emailinfo@bbcnc.org.uk World Wide Web page (URL address) http://www.bbcnc.org.uk

Cyberia – the UK's first Cybercafé. For £2.50 per half hour you can go and try out cybersurfing at 39 Whitfield St, London W1 (Behind Goodge St Tube and Tescos). They also serve coffee and pastries – worth a visit. See Easynet below for address and details of Web page.

Demon – Registration £12.50 and from £10.00 a month after that. 42 Hendon Lane, London N3 1TT. Phone: 0181 371 1234. Fax: 0181 371 1150. email sales@demon.net http://www.demon.co.uk

Easynet – Registration £25 and from £9.90 a month. Very easy installation software. Linked to Cyberia café. Phone: 0171 209 0990. admin@easynet.co.uk. WWW page http:/www.easynet.co.uk/home.html

There are numerous other service providers, and more are being added all the time – check first to see if you can get local call access – it may not be worth your while if you live a long way from a PoP.

JACKIE HARDY

Computer Aided Design - Creation

In the beginning was the number cruncher.
On the face of it darkness screened.
God had cold feet, terminal-user worry.
He searched the void, put in a warm boot.
God logged on, remembered the colon
and there was light.

Then came the word. And the word was God
was trying to jump before He could run.
Hands on, God pressed space, split-screened
heaven and earth from the waters. At the
interface God inserted disks, backed up the system
with a graphic display.

The package had chips with everything,
So God got bold, accessed the menu in colour;
blocked the earth with green, the seas blue;
entered fish and fowl. With another byte,
God updated fields, returned beasts, cattle
and creeping things.

He opened a window, watched them browse.
God saved beasts and cattle, scanned creeping things.
Somehow there were bugs in the system.
God reprocessed data, executed, maximised;
gave creeping things another pair of legs,
a sting in the tail.

Then God created first generation humans
in His own icon. To the female He gave
the second generation function, the womb,
so that she might be fruitful and multiply
even unto the millionth generation.
And He called her Wombman.

Then God copied the female, cut and pasted,
deleted the womb. And the male He called Man.
God scrolled through His work, monitored progress.
God saw that it was good and that His name
was in the hi-scores. Level six ended the session.
God logged off.

The Quantum Uncertainty of the Narrator

A Conference at the Science Museum on Mar 26th, 1994, organised by The Independent, *brought together practitioners of the arts and science.* ***Paul Mills*** *was there:*

What is science? What does it do? If scientists were asked the same questions about art, how would they answer? Would artists be interested in their answers? Are scientists professionally embarrassed by artists claiming knowledge of the sciences? What can the two say to each other about what each other is doing? During the art-science forum at the Science Museum in March last year chaired by Melvyn Bragg, an invited audience from both sides attempted to answer these questions and others. This was British intellectual society on display, but oh dear, the questions were too complicated.

We know what science does: it predicts; it is a method of investigating reality whose aim is to discover unalterable laws, to change hypotheses into hard data. The same can be said of primitive magic except that the laws of science are found by observable proof, by repeating an experiment whose result is always the same: material reality is, was, and will be this way: this happens, happened, and will happen. Whatever an atom is, do this to it and it reacts thus. Art, by contrast, is a leisure thing, soft: it comforts and uplifts (Louis Wolpert). But Goya isn't comforting, interjects Melvyn Bragg: really another question, but again, rather complicated.

Is it the case, as was suggested, that Science progresses, that Art is non-progressive, that Einstein or Heisenberg might replace Newton but not Shakespeare Sophocles? Although Milton is still a great poet his cosmology is not available to poets writing now in the same way as it was to him. Stravinsky replaces Mozart, and no one writing a novel now would think of trying to imitate Jane Austen. So of course the arts progress, of course artists find the conditions of each others' works unrepeatable. And so it went on: big generalities, as if the histories of science and art were formulae, theorems, rules which lift the final veil on the subject. 'The discoveries of science can never affect reality', Yeats wrote to Sturge Moore in 1926. Is this any longer an acceptable statement? If nature is a fabric whose interwoven threads and texts are vast but still decipherable, are not its observers part of the text? Might not the conditions in which observation occurs alter what is observed? Heisenberg's Principle of Uncertainty claimed just that and did so in the same year, 1926. Reality was affected by a discovery. The uncertainty principle of the quantum marked the break with classic Newtonian physics.

Any discussion which aims to bring the two sides closer together will need to resist this statement of Yeats and begin to think more seriously about uncertainty. Most people living in the dominant scientific culture of the present believe that the sciences can predict causes and effects within a certain field of operations. It is, for example, generally believed that there was a beginning and is going to be some end to the universe. The more that is understood about the forces of nature, the more will be known-about what happened in the beginning and about what is going to happen – this was the general doctrine according to Newton. But in the past half-century, the aim to predict events by observing them has been challenged within science. Quanta of light used for measuring particles in motion affect their behaviour in ways which are unpredictable. A particle appearing in one place may or may not be the same as the one seen vanishing from another. What happens in between these two events? And even assuming there are two events, can the track between be predicted? Is the aim of science still one of divination or has it changed?

In considering what the consequences of Heisenberg's principle might be for art, a problem arises which involves the question of the discourse, or discourses, available to the media through which the debates are expressed. If scientific discourse develops within the testing of propositions through experiment, can the term 'narrative' – which clearly would be borrowed from another – be valued within that discourse? Literary projects, poems, plays, fiction, criticism, frequently deploy discourses which clash; they are allowed to borrow registers from a range of institutionalised languages, and deliberately subvert the notion of distinct disciplines. Can terms such as 'proton', or 'quantum' only be used within the discourse of physics? To substitute 'process' for 'proton' brings the concept closer to 'narrative', but are such substitutions permitted within science? If not, the right to be heard seriously within that discipline could be forfeited, since knowledge is owned by the discourse and by the institutions which go on producing it. But does it matter very much if such a right is forfeited? How authoritative are such institutions, and are they becoming less so? Are terms such as 'particle' or 'wave' metaphors or literal descriptions of protons? Might not contradictory metaphors be applied to the same phenomenon? This is a problem for physicists, but one which may allow others to contribute. Franz Capra's book *The Tao of Physics* is one example of a new multidisciplinary approach to particle physics, and clearly it is impossible to stop terms, concepts and words with scientific origins from seeping into the common language and turning up in poetry and ordinary speech.

In an atmosphere where ideas are reviewed in new and strange combinations, it would be unhelpful to ignore the link between Heisenberg's theory and certain theoretical insights about narrative and structures of reading in contemporary thought. The concept 'narrator' suggests a position of knowledge, even if that knowledge is unreliable. But experiments in science (before and after Heisenberg) aim to make the scientist-narrator of events and phenomena reliable. If, however, in Heisenberg's theory, the position of reliable narrator remains vacant, since quanta of light prevent a completely objective observation of the 'story' of what happens to a proton, it does so in order to be filled at some point eventually. The narrative has to be changed by speaking of particles not as fixed objects but as waves.

Theories of narrative outside science are more accepting of narration being partial and unreliable. After Barthes, not even the author can control everything which might be happening in his or her text. And so it is, after Derrida, with narratives of history. Can the concept 'science' be the same in Newton as in Einstein? The same in quantum theory as in chaos theory? Both theories question narrative by questioning how it is measured, yet both might appear in a narrative called 'the history of science'. 'Science' may change into something 'not-science', or 'not-science-as-it-was', yet it's hard to speak of a difference without some reference to what 'it' – 'science' – was earlier. The word 'difference' can't help but suggest that some kind of step between is being narrated.

Uncertainty, and this is the whole point, does not give up on the quest for full knowledge and mastery of phenomena through science-narrative; instead it defers the position of reliable narrator. It has to do this because what it observes at one time, given the same set of circumstances, cannot be predicted for another. This gap in narrative is exactly what interests the newly developing positions in post-modernist thought, and exactly what leads to a mixing of disciplines and discourses on narrative. Reliable narrative can only be a narrative *afterwards;* it predicts events as if they were somehow known as having happened. But since Heisenberg there appeared, for the first time in science – the acute possibility that no narrative *afterwards* can be found. The drive for mastery implies a continual repositioning, ever more outside, beyond or above the previous angle of observation, in order to achieve the sought position of omniscience.

One of the most powerful and obsessive narratives has always been that of the story of creation, and the sources of authority for these narratives-afterwards were sacred texts, heroic epics, folktales, legends, and in the present, cosmological theories of the beginning and end of the universe, of the basic building blocks of matter and the forces of nature operating within and through them to produce gasses, stars, galaxies, and time itself, out of the primeval explosion. The search for this narrative ranges from observing the outermost galaxies, to the attempted discovery (authorised by massive financial investment) of indivisible particles within protons, to the unified theory of one single force, of which others – electro-magnetism, the gravitational force, and the nuclear forces – are facets. By the way in which this branch of science is currently being popularised, it seems that the dominant cultures which support it are constantly being promised some imminent discovery which will solve, as if for all time, the question of the fundamental nature of matter, of the extent and consistency of spacetime, of how it came to be as it is, and possibly even why. While it is tempting to ridicule these projects as wasteful and as motivated by the desire for mastery, it's surely important that, as a result of them, much is now known, if not yet all, of the vast regions outside of our own planet, and that some, if perhaps not quite all of this knowledge is accepted and envisioned as fact. Its perspectives are so huge and so staggering they almost prevent the very imagination they provoke.

That one single object, a quasar, can be the same mass as one hundred galaxies like our own, is as meaningless to the imagination as a heliocentric universe would have been in the twelfth century, and yet of even greater importance to contemporary science is the notion of matter as adjacent, as not constructed within a system of meaning. Science no longer *speaks of* anything outside or beyond its own discourse; moral, metaphysical, or value-termed discourses are omitted.

The consequence of science since the late Sixteenth Century has been to defamiliarise the world: it shows that an adult human body has grown from one single cell to trillions, that the furthest galaxies are an equally large number of light-years away from earth and consist of an equally large number of stars. But instead of microcosm and macrocosm, the terms macroworld and microworld suffice for an explanation, and indeed provide no explanation as to why things are the way they are, nor about what or who caused them or is reflected metaphorically in them. The problem now is that, in comparison with a world where poetry, myth, legend, epic, or sacred texts, developed stories with a transcendent significance or idea of moral guidance for human behaviour in the cultures from which they originated, the creation narratives of contemporary science do not come along with any such built-in moral or social implications. In effect, on matters of spacetime and the Big Bang, the originating event, there seems to be little in the popular imagination of the dominant culture beyond a mild and fleeting curiosity, and a few scattered impressions, none of which have any impact on belief or patterns of living. While creation narratives in the past did exert such influences ours does not. But why not? Might not science even now help us towards an understanding of nature based on value?

In recent times, science has served the popular media profusely. Rather than felt as estranging, space in culture has become peopled with legends, epics, stories featuring encounters with the divine or the diabolical, monsters, heroes, journeys to the unknown – as if the unknown were sited permanently 'out there' not down here. Who owns space? How does it signify? Space provides a throwback to some earlier, but now fictionalised picture of a moral universe, laced of course with a combination of ancient and modern technology, where Medieval costumes coexist with laser fire-power and neutron-destruction weaponry. Space is a panorama of old and new racial hatreds, Victorian notions of evil, sexual stereotypes, and all the narrative constructions which exploit them. The cosmic background – screen-space – is made use of continually, littered with products and credits; it provides the ultimate outline of high significance, while directing attention away from real space. All this preoccupation with screen-space is of course highly entertaining as well as increasingly lucrative, and is itself evidence of a form of post-modernity, since the once transcendent stories are now fictionalised – in a setting which both permits and undercuts them – by representing the antiquated alongside the contemporary. The number of TV studios featuring stars as a background for some award ceremony or gameshow spectacular suggests again how space is used to signify ultimates of fame, elevation, talent and affluence: the qualifying values of the dominant culture.

Concepts of space have a history. Space as mechanism: huge wheels with the symmetry of a clock. Space as sublime, inclined over and above us with biblical power, as in a vast canvas by Robert Martin, as the source of divine anger against the puny defences of a corrupt world. Space as the province of God – the fixed stars arranged on transparent spheres with earth at the centre. The sun and moon as male and female deities, as sources of fertility or infertility, the earth suspended between them like a cradle. The fierce sun and silent inquisitive moon, or the man-cursing moon pulling the sea and menstrual tides of women. The moon horned like an ox ploughing the earth. The hot moon of flagrant passionate romance. Stars in clusters with names of legend like Sirius, the Great Bear, the Seven Sisters. Star-influences predicting the time of birth and subsequent course of a life. All this has in its way no doubt been all very wonderful, very poetic, very transcendent. But now, unfortunately, it's time for all that to come to a very abrupt and conclusive stop.

What might be alternative ways of representing the impact of space? Such a phrase begs the question of whether anything called merely 'space' can have an impact on anything, but at this point I must make clear what my own position is, or rather, is not. It is not like any of the above. All these are narratives afterwards. They can indeed be made use of as narrative games, but not as trans-cultural signifiers whose aim is to impose meaning on present credible reality.

To explain its particular consequences, the new sense of observable limits in science needs to have its poetry (just as the old narrators did, of which Yeats was a powerful and recent example). To borrow Emily Dickinson's phrase, its business is circumference. To call such poetry post-scientific would be appropriate. It follows the drive of defamiliarising reality, but not that of explaining it in any grand complete unified theory, (to which it is probably temperamentally resistant), preferring partial narratives, wide perspectives, a sense of harshness, astonishment, amusement, and certainly incompleteness. A sense of incompleteness is crucial – more accurately, of uncompleteableness – in distinguishing the post-scientific temperament. Things appear out of nothing, by accident or as miracle, as real, but unexplained. The perspectives last briefly then vanish. Although this kind of writing is a matter of possible direction rather than already assured certainty, a lead might be found in the work of Miroslav Holub and Zbigniew Herbert, whose combinations of science-perspective, philosophy, partial narrative, religion, comic-ironic monologue, remove discourses from whichever institutions own them, and mix them aesthetically, without ever draining them of harshness, so that imagination, to quote from the words of Mr Cogito, rather than stoking the 'artificial fires of poetry' becomes instead the instrument of compassion.

In real space there is no story, or the story will take so long to unfold it reminds you that you only glimpse the tiniest fraction of it then you die. Yet the sense of glimpsing something - though what, you will never know - only that this something is reality, of being inside it rather than outside, which is where science has returned us: all this feeds the capacity for wonder, and for wonder without any other audience present. Life comes about and faces extinction in space, and no other versions of reality are waiting out there to tell us how the story will end or even why it happened. To see and respond to the lack of complete story surely develops art and writing as instruments of compassion.

Because of its tradition of addressing perspective and meaning through images, poetry is fitted to record the images which physics is bringing to bear on our present-day consciousness. These images dwarf the human figure and its mastery over chaos in human time. They show the presence of omniscient objective narrator – the classic position of physics before Uncertainty – as a ghost: the outline is a vacancy, the substance uninhabitable. If a dominant position was available before, it is now vacant. But why should poetry take on this issue? Why not fiction or drama? Why not indeed. All writing as art faces this incompleteness of vision which is also an incompleteness of form. Solutions and whole narratives are absent. Full knowledge of the background on all sides up or down is now impossible. Seen by writers or scientists willing to base their authority on a glimpse of this background, it is a fog, it is impenetrable. The attitude to this impenetrability is, nevertheless, ambivalent. The loss of access is itself one of the images: some would call it fuzzy logic or chaos. The world called up by art and science *is* now invariably foreground, however far it extends. However seemingly far they move towards clarity, the background is without access and even the foreground doubtful and subject to chance. Whoever survives wins, but winners, whether horses or species, are impossible to predict. We have no theory of weather or climate change, no theory of environmental disaster, by which all species now or in prehistory are randomly selected for survival. The word 'randomness' replaces 'natural selection' in the post-Darwinian world. Can we have a theory of randomness? Is Chaos Theory, frighteningly mis-named, a last attempt to find the comfort of order?

Without such comfort, this position of vulnerable semi-ignorance can make the facts of the foreground look odd, unfamiliar. Certain facts can borrow the feeling and quality of an image. How far, for example, is the Science Museum from space? About the distance of Dorking – fifty miles. If we convert this strange fact to a value we might say that anywhere on the planet, whatever it might signify to itself, is a mere fifty miles from uninhabitable void. What better antidote to the bold concept of nations or states as meaning, or to their blind squandering of resources

Against nationalist culture or racist religion, science can aid thinking in terms of species. To extend the foreground: how long would it take, travelling at speed on a motorway, to reach a star four light-years from Kensington? By my calculation about sixty thousand years, or several times the period representing civilisation. Looking back fifteen billion years the Hubble telescope or some future equivalent of it might see the beginning of time, but beyond that is a blur outside of physics. To draw the remotest regions into our foreground (the aim of radio astronomy) only draws closer the sealed up face of the wall. Probes loosen the interstices which re-form. If art challenges science, if science challenges itself, the terms resolve on the issue of incompleteness. These images might create bad poetry or good physics, or good poetry and bad physics, but the requisite adjustments can't be made unless the images of physics become objects of profound and prolonged contemplation, of the kind of attention which, in the past, it was the business of poetry to initiate. The images may become sharper, that is, specified with more impact, but the general impact is hard to ignore and may even be dangerous to iqnore.

To see this limited consciousness *as a value* – at its best limited but adjacent – will happen only if the limits are made clear and real as experience. That it has value means it must not be squandered or wasted or put in danger of extinction. It marks the onset of wonder and curiosity, and flawed though it is, there is no alternative consciousness. This state of alert explorative attention is worth something; it is a tiny flower in a desert of stones; it appears to be a profoundly rare, chance event in a sterile, motiveless system of infinite reach: an accidental mystery. To preserve its watchfulness, its sense of its own vulnerable incompleteness, we need both physics and poetry.

Paul Mills' latest collection is* Half Moon Bay *(Carcanet, 1993);* Writing in Action, *a resource book is forthcoming from RKP.

PASCALE PETIT

Ghost Leaves

They arrived mail order, twopence each,
enough to fill this box, to leaf one tree
– the sacred peepal, brother to the banyan,
a species of strangler fig with roots
that cling to the trunk of a host
forming an exoskeleton.

Also known as skeleton leaves.
Once dead, they fall with their veins
intact, the cellulose dried
to the colour of vellum. In India
they are used to paint miniatures
for weddings, funerals.

Scenes are depicted on a leaf shaped
like a heart, a thin dried heart
torn from its body with green blood
and green bloodcells which eat sunlight.
They lie in my box
eating the dark.

Their veins draw ghost-blood
from the great ghost-tree
also named the bodhi tree
where Gautama sat
and became Buddha, drawing enlightenment
from the green light of its leaves.

The stems encircled him
forming a lattice around his frame
– the matrix of an empty tree.
Forest denizens made short work of him.
Leaves sprouted from his bones.
An artist painted a thousand eyes on them.

He has been sitting for a thousand years
transforming light to oxygen.
Is Buddha in my box?
Is the hollow core of the peepal in my box?
If I unwound the ghost-veins of all these leaves
would they reach the sun?

But they are mooncoloured.
They give off a reflected glow like moonleaves.

They are eating moonlight to make airlessness.
They are making a moon atmosphere
here on earth, in my room, far from India.
Are the leaves cold, do they long for the rainforest,

their brothers and sisters, their extended families?
Have they been posted to the moon?
Can they hear the city outside my house?
The moonbox is in a room full of books.
Can they hear ancestors
buried in the books and wood of these shelves?

Is this the afterworld for forests?

SALLY CARR

Electrons on Bonfire Night

The night sky, if you ignore light-
pollution, provides the blackboard.
Strontium atoms for red, blue
from copper, sodium for yellow.
A physics lesson in the garden.

But it all happens so fast:
Roman Candles a one-minute
hallucination, rockets shot
from bottles, the crazed dazzle
of a Catherine Wheel. That smell,
remembered from childhood Novembers,
where a blinding Vesuvius,
Mount Etna or Golden Rain cascaded
and petered out. Tomorrow, the box
of charred remnants. And rocket sticks
found on the dustbin, and days later,
the largest one, on the shed roof.

Then we're left with the bonfire.
As it slowly craters to red,
our combined sparklers describe
the air in magical discs,
rhomboids, parabolas –
that are there and not there, collide,
loop the loop, expire. Laughter
and gasps replace whizzes and bangs.

Clean, like peals chiming against
frost air, our sounds make connections
beyond the tree shadows, the lit faces
and circle of smoke, somewhere
other than our half-comprehension.

The mechanics of unreality
happen all along: we only
have to make the leap. Tonight,
when physics is philosophy
and philosophy physics, we're
echoes on stars. Vanishings.
Returning murmurs in the universe.

Sally Carr won First Prize in the 1993 Bridport International Poetry Competition.

KEKI N. DARUWALLA

The Glassblower

He knew about glass and its history:
beads of the vintage of Amenhotep;
the Nineveh tablets of Assurbanipal;
blowpipe, maver, pontil, each successive step

Which fire took to make clay transparent.
'Glass is not in the family', he said.
'My forefathers were alchemists, sublimators
of baser alloys like zinc and lead;

believers in a four-cornered universe
of water and air, earth and fire.
They spent a lifetime with bellows, furnaces.
They were metallurgists, but they aspired

to mysticism. Alchemy for them was not
some quack technique harnessed to greed of wealth.
The goal was transmuting the earthy
to the celestial, sickness into health.

Now things are changed; a philosophy slips out
as an age loses its teeth. Nothing holds fast.
Decay sets in with birth:
we rust like iron, we splinter like glass.'

We walked past litter to his boiler room
where a reed-thin boy in a tattered vest
and a lost face dipped his blowing iron
into a small vat of silica paste.

The furnace, fitted with fire-clay pot and flue,
crackled and hissed. The stilt legs of the boy
glowed faint red on the shin bone as he put
the blowing iron to his lips and blew.

His cheeks turned to hemispheres, fully blown;
his neck, corded and veined, struggled till the nape
with his exhalations. A blob balooned
at the pipe's other end and froze into shape.

A smell of burnt resin, fossil gum, miracles,
of just fallen lightning came from the bowl,
as it should, with clay altered to replicate
the luminous transparencies of the soul.

The first time men saw this state of mist,
this veil that veiled nothing – O glorious deception –
and glass cool into colour of space, did they cry out:
'This is no object, it is thought, perception!'

Keki N. Daruwalla's latest collection is *Landscapes* (Oxford University Press, 1987).

AMANDA WILSON
The Double Helix

So we had lunch, telling ourselves that
a structure this pretty just had to exist'.
James Watson.

We measure ourselves like this:
there are two of us; we have two daughters.
That's even odds against loneliness.

The nuclear family on television, advertising
something – lean beef, or cereal –
two plus two round a table. Pairs in a match

not sparring – but smiling – exchanging syllables.
Breathing the common air and the common water
as though the world depended on this

for happiness. It's the double helix in us:
the idea that assent is delightful.
So we walk around, saying, 'Aah!' admiring the model.

But there is defection in us
deeper than the twining structure –
that doubling and re-doubling, never ceasing. . .

The daughter damns her inheritance.
The parent smashes the mirror. The lover turns
off with a beautiful, private wrong

we are coldly glad of. An odd equation wrenches
the double image off
its axis –

divergence –
single –
savage!

Amanda Wilson is an Australian poet whose work has appeared in many Australian magazines.

JOHN GOODBY

Soho

I never thought of a Girl as a possible event ...
however, I bore the sex with great fortitude.
(Coleridge, letter to Southey)

The map had misled him all round the Wrekin.
When he asked his road at the cottage door
a hag appeared whose ugliness was soul-gelding
enough to chill a cantharidized satyr

to eternal chastity. But angel choirs
of light could hardly have been more civil
to a Pantisocratic Unitarian devil;
next day he dripped manna for seventy score –

sky-blue topcoated, lank hair unpowdered –
where King and Country mobs had smoked Priestley out.
Even his fleas were citizen-philosophers,
emigrant live nits from a Welsh democrat.

He fanned the congregation to slippery heat,
yet lost a tallow chandler's subscription –
an entire morning's recital of 'Religious Musings'
quenched by a face as long as Livery Street

and 'Who watches *The Watchman* then? Spy Nosy?'
A Lunatic cicerone'd him to Hockley Brook
and the Soho Undertakings. They were stickier
than the snug in the Salutation and Cat. Sweat

dripped. Beam engines nodded dully. Cylinders spat.
He grasped his thought like water; this was steam,
it hissed insinuation: 'I offer what
the whole world desires, Sir – power'. And if

the Condenser was Faith, the Governor Hope,
Charity a Parallel Motion . . .? Steam embossed
and blistered the seal of a note from Stowey
he had pocketed unread from the morning post

that began, *Dearest Samuel* (like her,
Sun and Planet gears seemed to revolve his name,
cogs tooth-kissing), *the midwife just came*
in time to take away the afterbirth.

***John Goodby's work appears in* Faber Introduction 8.**

JOHN LATHAM

The Unbearable Weight of Mercury

Quince, quina, quila, quiddity.....
A wax-bead topples off the candle-stick
limpets on his finger inching up the page.

His dictionary, lifetime's work, complete
except for this last entry that so troubles him
side-stepped years ago with:
'Mercury. See quicksilver'.
Now he can procrastinate no more: he thumbs his notes.

Extraction: Condensed out of vapours from roasting calomel
or cinnabar's vermilion crystals.

Healing agent: For boils and other pestilences
pour a goblet-full into a muslin bag
immerse in boiling water
hold against the inflamed parts, ignoring all discomfiture.

Forecaster of wind and rain: Thirty gleaming inches
balancing the whole weight of the sky.

Signaller of agues and fevers: sealed thread
sensitive to heat or cold
placed snugly under tongue or in the rectum.

Conductor of the electric fluid: Metal shafts
dipped into pools of it, rotate smoothly without sparking.

Escapist: Tipped out of its jar, it scampers table-tops,
leaps like lemmings, tight parabolas,
nestles between floorboards, inextricable.

Coquette: Dazzles all eyes, slips away from touch.

Source of pleasure: Romans filled deep baths with it
lay upon its sheen with wine or slaves.

Source of pain: Poisoned mirror – Narcissus first to die.

Warning on the dark-blue bottle: Be sure it does not drip
into cavities or lesions, especially of the face.

Note from Rebecca when she left me: I cannot kiss a man whose mouth is a black graveyard.

Quetzal, quiblet, quick-bread, quicken . . .
The candle splutters, he dips his quill:
'Quicksilver. See mercury'.

LAVINIA GREENLAW

Akhmatova in Lambertville

The revelations of ice, exactly:
each leaf carries itself in glass,
each stem is a fuse in a transparent flex,

each blade, for once, truly metallic.
Trees on the hill explode like fireworks
for the minute the sun hits.

Fields hover: bleached sheets in the afternoon,
ghosts as the light goes.
The landscape shivers but holds.

Ice floes cruise the Delaware,
force it under in unnatural silence,
clarification I watch as I watch

the road – nothing but the grind of the plough
as it banks snow, drops salt and grit.
By dark these are just settled hills,

grains embedded in the new fall.
We, too, make little impression
walking back from town at midnight

on bird's feet – duck's feet on the ramp
where we inch and scrabble our way to the door,
too numb to mind the slapstick.

How did you cross
those unlit, reinvented streets
with your fear of traffic and your broken shoe?

There are mornings when it drips and cracks.
We pull glass bars from railings,
chip at the car's shadow.

Lavinia Greenlaw is currently Writer in Residence at the Science Museum, London.

PETER HOWARD

Poetry for Scientists

(after Lavinia Greenlaw, *mutatis mutandis*)*

We take a cab to your flat
on a Saturday afternoon. Those cultured brain-cells
have spawned an idea, and you must feed them.

Your wife makes us welcome.
With its comfortable air, kids' toys, and flowers,
I'm surprised by your room. Sure, there are

books on shelves
and enough scattered papers to make me
nervous of sitting down, but on the table

sits the latest cellular telephone,
and next to the word processor
a fax stutters a sonnet.

You open the door of an ordinary fridge,
offer me a beer, but say
you drink nothing stronger than Perrier yourself.

I want a draughty garret,
tousled hair and Byronic eyes,
the threat of death by opium or razored vein.

I want an empty whisky
bottle, several mistresses, the grubby remains
of a week-old dinner on the draining board,

to catch sight of poetry
in the forceful crossing out of a half-completed
manuscript, to discuss the uselessness

of your contemporaries–
how x is over-rated
and y never fulfilled her early promise.

I miss the Thursday afternoons:
'honour rooted in dishonour', synecdoche
and zeugma with its odd initial letter.

Now, I watch you
turn on your dictation machine to record
each new idea, in search of a rhyme

or at least a word that fits,
or else in hope of some wild inspiration
that without your eye for an image, I'd certainly miss.

****Lavinia Greenlaw's 'Science for Poets' first appeared in* **Poetry Review** *Vol 82 No 2, 1992; it also appears in her collection,* **Night Photograph,** *Faber 1993.***

WILLIAM SCAMMELL
Solway Plain

First I talked with the mare and her foal
on my evening walk down the broad farm track,
bluffing her into a social call
with my foot on the gate, and layman's cluck.

She butts that huge, autochthonous head
at mine, and I don't know whether it's full
of brains, or friendship, or motherhood.
In fact I don't know horses at all

but we rub along for a minute or two
and I pretend to admire her son
whose skinny ribs are a poor first try
to the heft of his legs. Then I walk on

right past the solid dome of the wood
to the outstretched fields of the Solway plain.
It feels like nowhere, the back of beyond,
as though Tess might just blow through on the wind.

And there on the stubble young foxes play,
rushing and dawdling, all tail and eye,
three sorcerer's apprentices, to see
what kindles yet in a wisp of hay.

Then a whoosh! and the leap off the top of a bush –
breaking cover just above my head
a great tawny owl, who glared in the dusk
and wheeled off to the darkening wood.

Pale wild roses enlivened the hedge,
honeysuckle swam in the gloomy pines,
woodpigeons, clattering out of their lodge,
flapped me back to a meeting of lanes.

The mare had vanished. The farmer's wife
was yelling out, as he sheeted the bales
in Stygian plastic, each burly sheaf
wrapped up in Virgilian pastorals.

William Scammell's* Barnacle Bill *(Dedalus Press) came out last year. His* New & Selected Poems *will be published by Sinclair-Stevenson in the Autumn.

JOHN BURNSIDE
The Insect Station

In summer, when I come back to the house,
I find them:
butterflies, moths, a litter of perfect beetles
dead on the sill,
the wings of the lepidoptera
battered, or threaded with scales
like ash-flakes, or moonshine,

recalling that distant July, when I had
my first real job,
tending the tobacco moths and locusts
out at the field station, breeding them on
for lab work. I was the one
who vacuumed the cases, swept out the empty shells,
watered the beds of nightshade along the hedge,
the glasshouse of wheat blades, the border of yellow verbascum

– a dry year, like this: it felt like the edge of the world
just four miles out of the city, where no one would come
for days at a time, and I felt myself bleeding away,
sealed in the heat and the light, and the dry green smell
of fodder and larvae,
believing in something eternal, or endlessly
self-renewing, stubborn as the joy
that shapes each form
and grinds it out with passion.

John Burnside won the Geoffrey Faber Memorial Prize for* Feast Days *(Secker & Warburg); his latest book,* The Myth of the Twin *(Cape) was one of the 20 New Generation titles.

Redgrove's Incubator

Peter Redgrove outlines his working methods

The creative process has been well charted – but is still mysterious. There are basic procedures the artist can use to open up to the possibilities inherent in himself and the situation; yet the process can't be forced. Berlioz called it 'careful luck'. 'Inspiration' is thus a composite.

There is always an important unconscious component. Hard work is essential – and it is hard work – but the 'germ' of a piece may seem to come from nowhere, is plucked out of the air. Henry James described the operations of this unpredictable grace in his Prefaces. Creators also agree that work at certain stages has to be incubated: that is, it must be allowed to 'cook' out of view somewhere in the psyche. Next time one looks, at least part of the work may be finished, as though it had created itself.

There is, then, the germ to be caught, which infects one with the fever of the work, the active drafting, the conscious experimentation with words and phrases right down to the last comma and vowel; then follows as deliberate a decision to be patient, to lose the work for a time in unknown regions to see how it fares there; and afterwards, to fish it out again, like Dylan Thomas's 'Long-legged Bait', and find in one's nets – what? a pile of bones or a new-born child ...

More soberly, two components are clear: the tension of conscious work, and the relaxation that allows the work to speak for itself. It is best to cultivate a balance and pliability between these two in order to make the best use of one's creative powers; the artist must be adept at both phases of this two-way process of willing, and receiving, of work, and incubation.

I evolved my own system of work because I consider the creative process the most valuable of mental events, and I wanted to make the fullest use of whatever gifts I have. I believe that the process is evolutionary, whether it occurs in art, science or in human relations. Thus, it is 'Faust' which creates Goethe. It is in this way that I believe the creative process can be lived; for example, in answer to the old question 'When is the analysis finished?', that is, when is a person functioning properly, Von Franz gave her answer 'When that person lives in a continual state of active imagination'. And to the other old question, put to Rodin by younger artists, 'What do I do when I can't work?', the answer was 'Work at something else'. I wanted a method whereby there would always be creative work to do, always work-in-progress to be taken up. What I evolved is very simple, and like a 'cascade' process in chemical engineering. I have used it for about twenty years, and thus there is in existence, for that time, a complete record in this detail and moving towards this form, of every stage of creative process in all my work: poetry, prose fiction, drama and psychology. For the purposes of this sketch, I will speak only of poetic composition.

II

The 'germs' of a work are all about us. The world is full of creative suggestions: it is composed of them. Most of us are too busy in other ways to take up these ideas; the professional creator must be very open to them. They are found in chance observations, words overheard, sudden headlines, fragments of dreams, the colour of a dress glimpsed through a window. The artist who wants to make the most of his world must set down these hints and guesses, sudden clarifications, brief mysteries, unexpected openings. They are the basis for his sketchbooks or *Journal* (1) (see diagram), found objects for his studio. They are live things, he must catch them on the wing. He must at this stage not worry them to death. He must allow them to reside in his Journal, which is the lobby of his studio, so they can find their own space there, and establish their own presence. In my own Journal – the first stage of the process (though at any time a complete poem may strike) – I set down everything would like to remember, everything I would like to become part of me or my world, both friends and enemies, from life or book or newspaper or companion. I record there also that spontaneous cinema of poetry that comes from within in dreams and reveries.

I let my Journal grow over the months. Currently I use large foolscap notebooks. When the Journal is full I begin reading it again: three or four months will have elapsed. As everybody who keeps any kind of diary knows, it is astonishing how such a practice widens one's awareness. One is astonished at what one loses in the ordinary processes of recollection without benefit of diary. Themes, thoughts and feelings become visible which the ordinary jerky occasions of daily amnesia would have fragmented and blown away. One discovers continuities of observation which would otherwise have been lost for ever, messages to oneself which would otherwise have been ignored, perhaps something terrifying claiming notice before it decides to emphasise its message with a toothache or migraine, perhaps some subliminal dæmon murmuring endearments. The Journal becomes a jungle, inhabited by a whole natural history. Since I have created this jungle, now I must explore it. As I am a writer, I will do this by writing.

My next act, then, will be carefully to corral this fauna and flora in a second-stage 'imagery' notebook (2). I will copy out from the Journal the most sinewy images, the most voracious metaphors, the strange centipedes of thought walking with more legs than I could have predicted. I may have seen, and can now contemplate, because the occasion has been fixed in a phrase, 'a young man holding in on leashes a pair of Alsatians like holstered and loaded pistols', and as I contemplate him, his whole past history may rise up before me, and why he brings these perilous beasts to a quiet wedding. 'Why' is his poem. I may think of how a person could lead another 'into her own secret wine-cellars'; I could establish in my mind the sheer 'legginess of a young cat drinking the dew off the cold window-glass, his eyes as he laps yellow as the yolks of two eggs'; I may *notice that I have noticed* 'how the fresh smell comes off the lawn just *before* the first drops of rain fall' or how the swan flies overhead with booming wings that rustle too as they thunder. Simply opening my eyes to some of these fragments and germs which would otherwise have been swept away on the currents of daily living may create a poem. I notice for example in an 'imagery' notebook of 1981 (71B I) that seeing how a clown's eyelids in makeup were 'cancelled with a cross' suddenly broke into twenty-eight lines on the antics of a circus as an allegory of death. These lines survived many drafts almost unchanged until the Secker volume of 1987 *(In the Hall of the Saurians).*

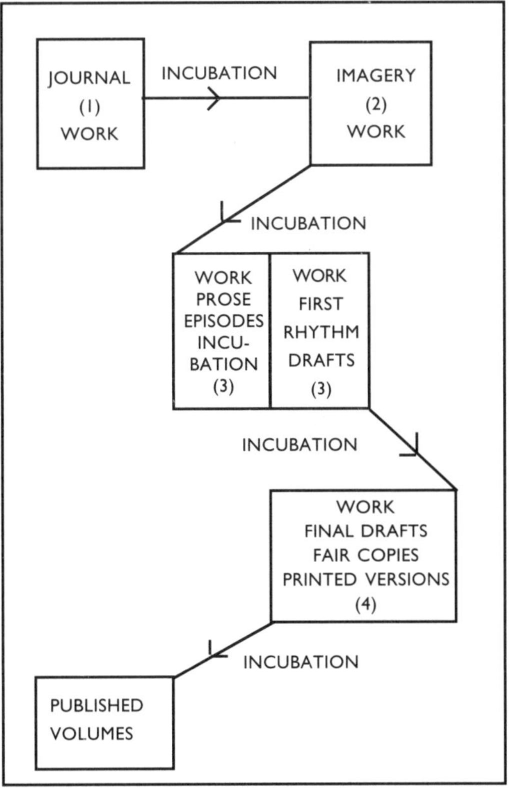

These are instantaneous moments of creation at an early stage; normally poems will need more incubation and more assembly than this. It is only after an interval of time that the second-stage 'imagery' notebooks are studied for the third-stage 'prose-episode-first-rhythm' notebooks (3). I have found that at this part of the cascade the revealed themes of the solid imagery set themselves quite naturally into short prose pieces (which are pasted on to the left hand pages). Why a prose draft for each of these many poems? Maybe it just happened; maybe I was following the great example of Yeats; maybe the prose rhythm is the first *sound* the fragments take up, their first intuition of connected voice, cry or howl. However it may be, this third stage notebook continues to capture its stories until the last left-hand page is reached, then it is put aside. After an interval, it is opened again, and, with 'careful luck' the diary magic has happened again, and the prose episodes have learnt further speech. Some of course will have succumbed, and say nothing; others crowd forward to the next stage (though it is not unknown for a sequence of poems to take full form at the prose stage, thus being seen as prose-poems: there is, for instance, an 'Alchemical Journal' composed during the last 2-3 years which is about to be published).

This stage or platform in the cascade then is to reopen the same 'prose-episode-first-rhythm' notebook after the interval for the diary magic to work, when the prose episodes will be found to have taken voice (as described in the last paragraph). In this voice will be (with luck and attention) a tighter rhythm, more dramatic and declaratory than the prose, in which certain words and syllables must be omitted and others brought forward. At this stage the poem begins to sing, to require phrasing and lineation, which I give it, to the best of my capacity. The resulting 'first-rhythm' draft is pasted on the right hand side of the third-stage notebook (3) opposite its prose counterpart. When I have drafted and altered this first-rhythm version and taken its song or recitative as far as I can, then, again, I close this book and allow it to incubate.

When I open this book for the fourth stage, the poem must step up out of its pages of its own accord, for the next book is for *final drafts and fair copies* (4) the latter to be sent for publication, and the printed versions to be pasted at the back also: these will provide the material for the very final stage of all, the publication in volume-form.

I notice that the young cat belonging to my daughter, last seen in an image-fragment in 71B II (1 June 1986) has arrived with his legginess intact on p.325 of a 'final draft and fair copy' notebook (79: begun 3 Feb 87) ready for consideration for a new Secker volume: 'A cluster of drops scuds down the glass/And shatters on the sill, his paw darts out/And inquisitorially turns the meagre/Water over and over – and then his tongue/ Darts out and swiftly laps it up,/The innocent water which squeals with light'.

The swans, however, of 1981 (71-B I) go on booming, and the fresh smell of the grass just before the rain rising to the nostrils, in a poem called 'Word' in the 1985 RKP volume *The Man Named East and Other Poems* (pp.89-91).

Peter Redgrove's archives are available for study at the Sheffield University Library.

MAURICE RIORDAN

The Real Thing

We live inside a steady atomic bombardment
where everything emits corpuscular streams of images
and so conveys colours, shapes and noises to the senses
– according to the unified theory of Lucretius
who killed himself, we're told by Saint Jerome, when sickened
by a love draught, by love gone wrong, so to speak,
in its chemical form; having by then composed,
during the catastrophic last years of the republic,
De Rerum Natura, the nature of things or simply Nature:
which we know sensationally, first-hand, through the body.
Jerome, as you'd expect, approved the Roman's assaults
on pagan gods, as well as his most un-Roman-like
recoil from sexual love: so the poem found passage,
in one defective manuscript, into modern hands;

where it arrives still fresh with that heady first draught
of Attic speculation, as yet unhindered by results.
Nothing is beyond its range: the particles of matter,
magnets, dreams, physiology, earthquake, British weather,
the temperaments of the wild beasts and 'military use
thereof' . . .
It enquires into questions such as how it is we hear,
though we cannot see, people talking in the room next door;
why, as we bend towards a looking-glass, we see ourselves
rise from its depths. These are not 'thorny' questions,
Lucretius assures us: though lacking (as he must) the law
of incidence and reflection, and impossibly far
from any inkling of frequency or wavelength,
his hypotheses have here the demonic gleam of de Selby
with something of a small boy's ingenuity and charm.

But on the phenomena themselves he is vivid
and exact: we see the woodcutter on a far-off hill
raise the axe to shoulder level, even as its report
reaches the ear; shadows walk beside us in the moonlight;
we bend above a puddle that reflects the heavens;
those heavens open and discharge their hail; the air splits
and we smell – as we never have in life – the alien,
sulphurous stench of a house gutted by a lightning bolt.
Or he can be sweet. Then the stiff hexameter swells
with brave notions, gentle expressions: the pear-tree
gathers through its whole gnarled form the essence
of the pear and presents its flesh to the appetite;
cows roll in pasture, heavy with milk oozing from their dugs
('undiluted milk', he writes, to make the sucklings 'tipsy').

Here then is nature's peaceful traffic: Mars lies asleep
in Venus' lap absorbing her moist, maternal atoms . . .
Yet when he speaks of human love, it is 'incisions',
'stings' and 'loss of strength'. Even as the eye is drawn
to the radiant, volatile surfaces of girls or youths,
we're warned off ; and when the symptoms mount from cuts
and bruises to inflammation, delirium, unquenchable fire,
we're told 'distract yourselves with substitutes'
or else: *Sleep alone* – by this bewildered epicure
(deranged, the Fathers claim, from an overdose of potion)
who, in refrain, recollects his childhood home, the nights
he lay awake watchful of the Etruscan images
and having dreamt, perhaps, of Iphigenia;
a bookish, high-strung boy frightened by the gods

who would complete a lifetime's scientific effort,
not with ebullient strophes to Venus or Apollo,
but with the Plague of Athens, 430 BC
– in this to prove himself fit for mortal combat,
the poet of the vulnerable body: when the atomic cloud,
wind-borne off Egypt's salty marshes, invades the throats
of the citizens; carrying the weapons of cold and heat;
imposing a regime of thirst and hunger; which attacks
the citadels of life, whose seat – located in the breast –
totters but still holds; exquisite instruments are brought
to bear; and no relief, except in prayers and outcries.
Then not even those; the lively atoms have found
the tongue, 'interpreter of the mind', and disconnected it.
Nothing now but unutterable pains. And so it ends.

Maurice Riordan's first collection,* A Word From the Loki *(Faber), is the Poetry Book Society Choice for Spring – it is reviewed on p.30.

Metred Healthcare

As part of its National Health of Poetry programme, the Poetry Society is is investigating the actual therapeutic effects of verse. ***Dr Robin Philipp*** *is looking for hard clinical data; Mike Sharpe takes poetry into the world of psychiatric day care:*

Some of the links between poetry and health were explored by David Hart, Literature Officer, West Midlands Arts, in *Poetry News*, Summer 1992. They, and the role of Creative Writing deserve further debate. For example, Graham Greene once wrote: 'writing is a form of therapy; sometimes I wonder how all those who do not write, compose or paint can manage to escape the madness, melancholia, the panic fear which is inherent in the human situation'. The therapeutic uses of literature are, though, not widely recognised. Yet medicine and poetry were seen by the Greeks as having a common source of inspiration in that Apollo presided over both the arts, and Shelley even wrote, in 'A Hymn of Apollo': 'All harmony of instrument or verse, all prophecy, all medicine are mine'. Like John Keats before him, the contemporary doctor-poet Dannie Abse has suggested that poetry is an escape from the reality of the external world into the reality of the internal world. At the 1993 Cheltenham Festival of Literature, he reported that imaginative daydreaming is an escape from the precipitous pessimism of living or dealing with problems and the sphere of sorrow, and that it is used to restore 'balance'. As Chris Meade noted in *Poetry News* last year, 'the poem can articulate a personal vision'. Poetry has also been likened to medicine in that like the physician, the poet tries first to grasp, then to control the reality of the human predicament. Lord Russell Brain, a neurosurgeon, reported that: 'the poet uses words to evoke images and images to move and delight, new combinations of words to shock the reader into new experiences, or to revivify old ones, to excite pleasure by virtue of rhythm, rhyme and assonance. Moreover, for many people the rhythmic content of poetry can have a soothing effect.

But could, or does, reading or writing poetry benefit health, and do doctors, or should they, encourage patients or try themselves to express thoughts as poetry? In January 1994, we asked these questions in the *British Medical Journal.* Our enquiry identified several creative writing support groups, a Poetry Therapy Society in the USA, and several published anthologies of poems by doctor-poets. We also learned that doctors have read poems at night to help calm agitated patients, used them in medical education as a basis for debate, and quoted from them to help patients develop coping strategies at times of personal crisis. They have also been utilised in valedictory addresses, and for emphasis. For example, in his inaugural address, one Professor of General Practice quoted Robert Burns' poem, 'To A Louse', to note that if we are to respond to the needs of our communities we must listen to our patients' views and 'to see oursels as ithers see us'. The Clinical Dean of the Medical Faculty, University of Bristol, in his oration at a recent honorary degree awarding ceremony, commented that 'we are looking for those who, in the words of William Wordsworth, can provide: ÷those obstinate questionings of sense and outward, things√'. The British Medical Association Chairman, writing in a national newspaper in 1993 about the health hazards of scientific and technological advances, quoted George Crabbe: 'Man who knows no good unmix'd and pure,/ oft finds a poison where he sought a cure'.

Recently, a few poets have begun to work closely with General Practitioners and at least one GP has commented that poems could be included in annual practice reports. Another has suggested that for research purposes, medical students and doctors could be asked to express their feelings in poetry during or after a consultation. The poetic imagery from inviting patients to write and illustrate poems about their experiences of trauma, illness, and hospitals is also evocative. For example, one 15-year-old in-patient wrote several cautionary tales about the circumstances of his accident and sold them around the hospital. In the upheavals of new discharge policies into the community a long-stay psychiatric patient wrote: 'Have I Got To Go Somewhere', to express fears of having to leave a safe haven that for her was home. And when asked by the hospital teachers to do so, long-stay children in hospital have written some delightful acrostics from letters spelling the word 'hospital'.

The Czech immunologist–poet Miroslav Holub commented that: 'emptiness begins where the limits of man expand and contract'. Indeed, one of the tasks of the health professions is to help people combat widely experienced feelings of emptiness and of anomie, alienation and anonymity. As with therapies involving music, art, drama and play, encouragement with creative writing can help some patients to structure, organise and articulate their thoughts, feelings and emotions. Responses from the public to our enquiry in the *British Medical Journal* have included comments such as: 'to have to write emotions and feelings helped me understand how I felt and why'; 'poetry is infinitely preferable to a pill, has no adverse side effects and revitalises and enhances the human psyche'; and, 'reading poems is inspiring, therapeutic and calming'. Other research in the USA has even suggested that creative writing therapy leads to enhanced immune responses in the body and increased resistance to infection. With the Poetry Society and the WHO Regional Office for Europe, we are now exploring who, and for what problems, poetry therapy might be appropriate, and how any identified health problems might be met. We welcome comment on, and collaboration in, this work.

Dr. Robin Philipp is Consultant Senior Lecturer in Public Health Medicine and Occupational Medicine, and Director, WHO Collaborating Centre for Environmental Health Promotion and Ecology at the University of Bristol.

Water Orton! Water Orton!

by Mike Sharpe

'Almost any man may like the spider spin from his own inwards his own airy citadel.' This is John Keats' view of creativity expressed in a letter to his friend John Reynolds on February 19th 1818. In the same letter, he draws a distinction between the merely mechanical 'knowledge' of memory and the creative 'knowledge' that memory can release.

For the past two years, I've been working in several Psychiatric Day-Hospitals as a visiting writer running 'creative writing' sessions for patients (or clients) to help them release something of this creative knowledge.

Recently, this work has been under the auspices of *Gofal Celf* or Arts Care, a project in West Wales designed to provide a planned programme of artistic activities for mentally ill people in day-care centres and hospitals.

It's always rather surprising that people so readily sign-up for an activity with the label 'Creative Writing'. It's an off-putting title but there's no really adequate alternative. No title quite fits this particular pen-in-hand activity and, in any case, nobody else seems as sensitive as I am about the name. For many who attend, it's simply an activity that's not woodwork or art or kitchen-management.

And yet it's so much more. There's an enhancing magic about it which shows itself unbidden and so unexpectedly.

For an hour or so people sit at tables absorbed in something that they last did, probably with great reluctance, in their English lessons at school. And here they are, in adulthood, finding a new impetus to language, a willingness to struggle on paper with words, in a process that might have been left permanently impaired by the inhibitive nature of the formal education some of them have experienced.

It sometimes takes repeated assurance to take away the diffidence or embarrassment caused by 'I can't spell'. In some cases I've acted as an amanuensis where the problems of written English were too overwhelming. But that service has been needed only temporarily, until I've managed to persuade the writer that it's the ideas that matter not the means. Once that blocking is removed, the release is expansive, like taking off tight corsets.

A session is like a pool of quiet. There's nothing to disturb us, no urgency, no pressing demands or responsibilities. The world is outside somewhere and excluded. Memory and imagination are free to range unpressured and unchallenged. How rarely do any of us find ourselves in such a circumstance!

We focus for a while on a poem, a painting, a photograph, some music. After that, there's no intervention until, quite spontaneously it seems, the writing is complete and we wait a few minutes for the others to finish. Then comes the fun (or tears sometimes) of reading out what we've written. There's amazing respect for each other's writing simply because the experience of life that has brought us together means that sincerity is never undervalued.

Once there's trust, there can be confidence. And then the journey really begins. That's exactly what it is, a kind of travel-writing over a planned route with occasional pauses over points of interest. But the journey is internalised and private, not shared until it's completed. (I've yet to meet anybody unwilling to share what they've written.)

I remember on one occasion introducing Thomas Hood's bitter-sweet poem 'I remember, I remember' (not, incidentally, easy to find these days). I'd hardly had time to hand round some copies when a rather shy member of the group suddenly began to recite it in that incantatory way school-learnt poems are often spoken. After many years, the words had surfaced again (to some spontaneous applause). I mention it because it illustrates everybody's instinctive relish for the moods of language. In my experience, it is manifestly possible to blend that pleasure in words with a rediscovery of the power that words can exercise.

Later in the session, in answer to the question, 'As you get closer, what do you see?' this is what Mary found:

A coal-bunker on a balcony
a gate that's child-proof with a lock
cracked putty at the window and bright red bricks
a green front door and lino on the passage floor
with skirting boards
and dark distempered walls
a metal boiling-tub
a medicine cupboard with a lock..

My job is simply to encourage the pursuit of those lit images that are hidden away. Once found and released they can float to the surface and, perhaps for the first time, be seen with astonishing clarity.

In later sessions, we might get involved in inventiveness and story-telling but not at first. Fiction requires a degree of detachment that doesn't come as readily as honest recall.

It isn't confrontational writing, the kind that aims to face head-on the distortions of illness. It is much more a reinstatement of the value or significance that thoughts and feelings possess, however 'imperfectly' expressed they may seem,

Indeed, there's no such thing as imperfection. Everything is made true by the very act of being given words. In this kind of writing there's simply no place for deception or fabrication. The creativity lies in the baffling chemistry of interaction between self, word and experience. Repeatedly, at the end of a session, we say in a kind of wonder: 'Just think, none of this existed an hour ago'.

I took in, one day, Edward Thomas's 'Adlestrop' to illustrate how a moment can be unexpectedly and unintentionally momentous. One member of the group took to the idea with enthusiasm. As a child, he frequently travelled by rail from Leicester to Birmingham (I think to his boarding school) and one station-sign captured for him all the associations that journey had. He would greet my arrival each week with the cry:

Water Orton! Water Orton!
My Adlestrop!

I don't think he realised he had an Adlestrop before he discovered the possibility in Edward Thomas's poem.

Mike Sharpe has published poems in* Poetry Wales, Stand, *the* Spectator *and other magazines.

MARION LOMAX

First Lessons

I have learnt to walk
with fear on a leash:
it used to snarl at the door
every time I tried to leave.
Now it trots quietly
on impacted earth,
and sometimes it sleeps.

I'd forgotten how minds
can be open to the sky
with no overhanging boulders –
what it feels like to lie
stretched in damp, warm grass
with insects in my hair –
and the way you can hear
minute thrusts of plants.

I have perfected
throwing anger to gulls
who mew it back to sea,
and I marvel that sleep
saunters down from the high trees
to spirit you up there –
leaving the room without
opening a window.

Marion Lomax's first collection,* The Peepshow Girl, *was published by Bloodaxe in 1989.

Swansea UK Year of Literature

To mark this year-long festival, we celebrate with Welsh poets new and established. For details of the ongoing programme, ring 01792 652211.

GWYNETH LEWIS
The Reference Library

(To open the Sixth-Form Library at Ysgol Gyfun Rhydfelen)

Elsewhere a leather-bound volume holds the sum
of what a distant century knew
of cosmology and Christendom,
of how to cook with feverfew;

how to make silk; how Latin spread
like roads across a kingdom which then fell
to rhetoric and laws and lead
but let prophetic fishes tell

their older stories, ones of mortal sin,
how men of rock were spawned from tors
with tongues of granite, breathing whin
which stopped the logical conquerors.

How comprehensive! Look around you now:
concordances are a thumbnail wide,
a wafer-thin thesaurus shows you how
new languages are regicides;

there are directories of heads of state,
files of disease with their listed cures,
transport technologies to contemplate,
anatomies of the urban poor . . .

But compared to you, an encyclopædia
is thin provision. Throw the big tomes out,
and the almanacs with their logorrhoea.
Read first the lexicons of your own doubt,

for in your spines and not in those of books,
lies the way to live well, the best library;
for the erudition of your open looks
shall turn old words to new theologies.

Gwyneth Lewis was one of* Poetry Review's *New British Poets in 1987; her first full collection in English,* Parables & Faxes, *was published by Bloodaxe in March.

DERYN REES-JONES
It Will Not Do

It will not do how stupidly you love her and how stupidly that stops you loving me.
How my sparkling deconstructionist account of Eloise and Abelard, my laugh,
The fact I've learned to scuba dive and mountain climb, cook *cordon vert*
Without a hitch, run marathons and win, that I'm a babe
To die for, locust free, the kindest, loudest, randiest lover you swear
You've ever had, who teases, argues and agrees, who lets you do
Exactly what you like and when, who doesn't nag, or hate or scorn,
But keeps her dignity and more. It will not do, the fact I drive so fast
I make you lose your breath, that I can squeeze my car inside the smallest space
While putting lipstick on without a smudge, that when we dance
We're never out of tune. That I've a body known to make men weep.
It will not do that I can read your thoughts, your palm, your horoscope,
Your tarot, and your tea, anticipate your every move, that I can tell you everything
You'd ever want to know about yourself or me. It will not do
That I don't shout or cry or rant or plead, show you
The door marked exit that I ought, that I can kiss you till the cows come home,
But still, by not being her, can't kick you into touch. This repetition, even,
Both our strange compulsions to repeat, just will not, will not
Do. And it will not do that it will not do, that even if I were to fall in love
With you again, it simply just won't do that I'm not her
And would not, do not, must not, could not, will not, do.

Deryn Rees-Jones' first collection,* The Memory Tray, *is reviewed on p.63

JEAN EARLE
To Vera's

Faceless Vera.
Your ambience, somehow
The colour of plums . . .

Your room.
My mother drawing me up
Endless stairs. *My little legs, Vera . . .*

The sudden light. Laughter and tears
Ricochetted off walls.

Tongues of reproach, ley-lines,
Crimes of the dead. How did I know this,
Having no language but my needs?
By the tenderly stroked,
Bitterly pricked fur of their tones.

Your bed, Vera . . .
Deep, white. I trampolined
Till I was tired.

Then – the chocolate –
Always just one, huge –
Jelled up my mouth
With rapturous gloy. Who *was* Vera?
Ought I to remember
Any of those people?

Bounce: and bounce, bounce,
At the tall window,
Mad with light. A bird
Floated between myself and cars,
Miles below.

Vera, with no face, plum-soft,
Plum-rich. Your wound
That I had no word for? All these years
I have recalled, each feather plain,
The back of the bird.

Jean Earle's forthcoming collection,* The Sun In The West, *will be published by Seren this year.

On The Bus

Ian McMillan on new books from Seren

Deryn Rees-Jones,
The Memory Tray,
ISBN 1 85411 116 7
Catherine Fisher,
The Unexplored Ocean,
ISBN 1 85411 106 X
Tim Liardet,
Fellini Beach,
ISBN 185411 115 9
all published by Seren Books at £5.95

Here are three remarkable books from a press that's often regarded (or disregarded) as regional and somehow not quite On the Bus. You know the bus I mean: the poetry bus that's Going Somewhere. Well, this lot are definitely On the Bus, on the top deck looking out at the world and telling the driver which way to go.

I first read these books months ago, and then when I found I hadn't got such a tight deadline I put them down and turned to other things. (Specifically, a schools TV science programs about Ellie the Electrode.) Now, reading them again, the books are still fresh, still exciting. Some books of poetry are like Pork Pies: two days after they come out of the oven they're inedible. These books aren't pork pies.

Deryn Rees-Jones

Deryn Rees-Jones is the pick of the crop: a magician with attitude, pinning ideas down but at the same time giving them time to breathe, which isn't easy, as a visit to any workshop will testify. 'Shadowplay', for instance, is a love poem of delicate and child-like sensibility: 'You hold my head in your hands/ As if it were a globe/ Rocking me slowly/ From side to side. As if love/ Were a country/ difficult to place'.

The poems try to riddle out an identity from a vividly remembered (and imagined) childhood; in 'Half Term' the poet recalls a visit to a mysterious one-breasted Welsh-speaking aunt: 'Much later, to the click of a clock/and the soft night noise of street and sea,//my dreams came sleepily/ like sloppy slippered feet as Nesta//in a long white dress moved spookily, hiding her nakedness, the terrible lopsidedness/ of only one breast'. I love the child's (again!) language of the 'sloppy slippered feet' and the adult/children's image of 'the terrible lopsided-ness'.

There are a number of outstanding individual poems in the collection that, if there's any justice, should be widely anthologised in years to come: 'Lovesong to Captain James T. Kirk' for one: ' O slick-black-panted wanderer holding / your belly in, your phaser gun/ on stun, and eyes like Conference pears! You're not my type/ but I undress you, and we fuck,/and I forgive your pancake makeup and mascara, the darker shadows painted round your eyes'. Perhaps I'll go and deliver that at the next South Yorkshire Trekkies Meeting. Perhaps. 'Blue' is a reworking of 'Frank O'Hara-ish concerns in a Peter Sansomesque did this/did that *tour de force*: 'Noon in Greenwich Park. A freak heat-wave./ We've Take-Out from Pistachios and all around/ Mothers and children spreading themselves out under the trees and us,/ Out to Lunch. We are/ Laughing about Frank O'Hara. Lancashire./Talking LOVE, SEX, TIME in the hours before your train'.

Oddly, sometimes, the voice isn't so sure of itself: in 'Largo' the aunt who comes to teach piano has 'her emerald boa draped around her like a mutilated treble clef,/her loose false teeth clacking like a metronome', as though she'd been to Mars an the way to the lesson. These are hair splits, though. Deryn Rees-Jones is On the Bus. She isn't a pork pie. Ellie the Electrode isn't half as charged.

Catherine Fisher

Catherine Fisher's is a quieter voice. She also writes for children, and as often with the adult poems of children's writers, there's an enviable clarity of intent, purpose and execution. Some of the poems could almost be workshop kick-starters, could almost be for children but for a depth-through-simplicity that marks them out as something more: 'They are apples. Bite on hardness/ to the sweet core.// They are coracles; flimsy,/ soon overloaded.// They are candles. Carry them carefully. They have burned cities' ('Words'). This grasp of economy of language stands Fisher in good stead in the more ambitious pieces in the book such as 'Archaeology: Four Seasons', an album of impressions of a group of archaeologists, digging over a year, finding relics and also, without any hint of cliché, finding themselves: 'Speech is if, and when./ Speech is tomorrow./ Speech is what we will do,/ is red, heated,/ steaming and spicy'. By the Autumn of the year the answers may be forthcoming:/ 'Where we dig, we find ourselves,/whatever we look for'./

The answer came from the back,/ the girl wrote it down,// and it was a good answer too,/ though not to her question./ We looked at each other and smiled./ Next season we may start another field'. The most ambitious sequence in the book is the title piece, subtitled 'From the journals of James Hartshill, being an officer serving on His Majesty's ships Endeavour and Resolution. 1768-1799'.

The Unexplored Ocean sequence begins on a note of celebration and wonder as Hartshill writes to his wife back home: 'Charlotte, I wish you could see these people!/ Their ocean is blue, so blue, deeper than/ the gown you wore at Rookham;/ the splash and lift of it nudges the ship; their hills an uprush of trees/ mirrored in the calm lagoon where we lilt at anchor'. I think this is lovely descriptive writing, particularly 'the splash and lift of it', which is spine-tinglingly exact. Later in the sequence we move with Hartshill through a kind of Loneliness in Eden ('Yesterday I thought Of Charlotte, for no reason,/ sitting in the garden with the boys,/telling them of me, wondering where I am./ Their faces were blurs. Desire to see them/ made me grip the stays, an almost bodily pain'.) to an awful despair: 'We have explored, and everything has changed;/ we have gone too far and seen too much/ we have been forever sailing, sailing to this,/ and where do you go after deaths after striking that rock?'

Without doubt Catherine Fisher is On The Bus. Her poems are pork pies? I think not. Sparky as Ellie, I'd say.

Tim Liardet

Tim Liardet is a kind of odd-chap-out. You could fix Rees-Jones and Fisher in some kind of lineage: Rees-Jones from Carol Ann Duffy, Fisher with strong echoes of Gillian Clarke. Liardet seems to be all on his unfashionable own, though, and it makes his poems slippery. As I read the work, the image that springs unbidden into my head is of someone welding; the white heat, the goggles, the determination to make or fix. Slippery welding. Each poem is Written with a capital W, and of course that's no bad thing: 'The driver looks straight forward. To the left/ The cafe's smoking man rests his mouth/ The dummies disclaim clothes, in orange light./ To the right, on three screens: the late show host./ On twelve – as the three switch to violins – / Twelve diving whales drag down their twelve fins' ('Free Association'), taking a late-night-drive through a cold cityscape as an image to clarify a deeper coldness, I think.

It's hard to say it without sounding mawkish, but Liardet is very good at heartache; indeed one of his poems is called 'Lovegrief'. In 'Aubade' he risks sentimentality but wins, as he lies in a half empty bed: 'My hand strays out, and stops. By now unable/ To hear the church's blurred and punctual bell/ Guide you through fog and snow, in your distant bed,/ feel my touch-without-touch tracing your furthest,/ Invisible outline, like the wish to mend./ And more than the snow has started to descend'.

I don't want to make Liardet sound like a Slim Volume Charley Pride, but it's good and rare to see hearts on sleeves in such a crafted way.

Ian McMillan's latest collection,* Dad, the Donkey's on Fire *(Carcanet), will be reviewed in the next issue.

KATHY MILES
Connections

It wasn't your dream that burst the night,
but still you held me, stroked my hair,
smoked out a lingering monster.
Such nights, I thought, had blown away
and would not come again this side of sixty.

We are mad with January gales,
the wind-chill of a long cold journey.
Storms that charge the air with something live
transform us from the calm of winter frost
to violence, heat, the shock of summer lightning.

I am all-electric. Switch on at a touch,
sleep like a dead sun in the dark.
My roots a mass of wires and cables,
alive to light, the right connection,
diverted by a memory swift as current.

Not for me the untidy ways of living:
fire's perpetual motion in the grate.
Old rites of candle-wax and shadowed hands,
the hurricane lamp or essence of oil
the priestess stirs to find a subtle message.

The time inside me moves too fast,
and I am slow and drowsy with my age,
discharge my energy in neutral ways,
am trapped by contacts in a circuitry
that's incomplete: an old, recurring nightmare.

Kathy Miles' first collection,* The Rocking Stone, *was published by Poetry Wales Press in 1988.

PAUL GROVES
Hypothetical

What is the next poem that you would have written
  Had you survived?
Something about your family perhaps,
  Postmodernist Britain,
The street where you lived, the farm where you'd thrived?
  Since your collapse

As father, husband, colleague, friend
  Your pen has lain still.
The stable is empty; the stallion you tethered
  Escaped. Your sad end
Is well documented, sobering, chill.
  The facts have been gathered.

If you returned, even after this time,
  How changed would you be?
Would you run down the street with a Lazarus grin,
  Ring the door-chime,
And startle your widow and children? All three
  Would welcome you in

With stunned disbelief. A whiff of the grave
  Or urn would attend you.
You'd need a good shower and fresher attire,

Not to mention a shave.
It might take some effort for them to befriend you.
In front of the fire

In your favourite chair you'd outline your trip
To the back of beyond,
How it all seemed a dream from which you'd awoken,
An abnormal blip.
Could the ripples return to the stone in the pond,
Its surface unbroken,

The missile unthrown? A playful conceit,
Like wool to a kitten,
For no one's returned, and nothing's arrived
Down the born-again street.
What *is* the next poem that you would have written
Had you survived?

Paul Groves' new collection,* Menage à Trois, *will be published by Seren in the Autumn.

JOHN POWELL WARD
Follow the Foliage

(For Morris and Sue Schopf)

An American philosopher
Wrote under trees, so it is said
In this encyclopedia.
Mauve, yellow, burnt sienna, red,
The autumn leaves fell round his head
Like fancies chasing round his head.
It was Thoreau. One day this man

Read how the Buddha picked some leaves,
And showed his followers and said,
'The forest's foliage, next to these,
Is all the thoughts I could have said.
Those were just some.' Last year in Maine
All my New England colleagues said
Follow the foliage. So we did.

Next year we followed it again.
Hourly reports on radio
Broadcast the turning leaves. A day
Can set the maple trees on fire
In orange tongues, and from your car
You kind of see the waves recede
Like daylight full of clouds at speed

In wave on wave, a week or more
Chasing them up to Canada.
The birch leaf goes a rustier red.
The tulip leaf is like a spade.
I guess I'm no philosopher.
We saw a million leaves last fall
And no thought bothered us at all.

John Powell Ward's latest collection is* A Certain Marvellous Thing *(Seren, 1993).

PAUL HENRY

Double Act

It's only a passing hum,
the waste collection.
We leave before it's come

or after it's gone,
or precisely at the time
the sacks are taken away,

or not at all; calm,
breathless, holding out
the ghost of a note

in each other's arms –
Ray and Renie Gray:
Children's Magicians,

Distance No Object.
Speciality:
Birthday parties.

Still pulling albinos
out of love's top hat,
still up to the act.

A tortured dove crows
under a purple sheet.
Look. Or go blindfold.

The King and Queen of Hearts,
still not too old
for the black arts.

Down time's sleeve,
fallen . . . fallen . . .
onto this huge bed,

a flick of the wrist
and now you see us
suddenly white-haired –

Ray and Renie Gray:
Distance No Object.
Keeping the van and the phone,

holding on to that smile,
the *Yellow Pages* ad,
avoiding the pot-holes

along the dark road,
for fear of vanishing
into them.

*

After the flaccid wand,
the silent gun,
the naughty kiddies,

after the last light-switch
of the last, echoing hall
of the last function,

a warm hand,
Ray and Renie: two halves
of the same soul,

a wave, a flurry, a kiss
and this . . . and this . . .
and this . . .

Paul Henry's first collection,* Time Pieces, *was published by Seren in 1991; his second collection,* Captive Audience, *is due from the same publisher later this year.

The Classic Poem

DANNIE ABSE

I FIRST HEARD this mature love poem on the radio scores of years ago. Its two sentences, its slightly unexpected syntax, its heightened conversational tone and its few memorable images have remained with me ever since. I'm not sure how particularly zealous feminists might react to the poem. Never mind, it was the poem that made me turn to Bernard Spencer, a poet of the 1930s, now too much neglected.

Dannie Abse's latest collections are* Selected Poems *(Penguin) and* On the Evening Road *(Hutchinson).

BERNARD SPENCER
Part of Plenty

When she carries food to the table and stoops down
– Doing this out of love – and lays soup with its good
Tickling smell, or fry winking from the fire
And I look up, perhaps from a book I am reading
Or other work: there is an importance of beauty
Which can't be accounted for by there and then,
And attacks me, but not separately from the welcome
Of the food, or the grace of her arms.

When she puts a sheaf of tulips in a jug
And pours in water and presses to one side
The upright stems and leaves that you hear creak,
Or loosens them, or holds them up to show me,
So that I see the tangle of their necks and cups
With the curls of her hair, and the body they are held
Against, and the stalk of the small waist rising
And flowering in the shape of breasts;

Whether in the bringing of the flowers or the food
She offers plenty, and is part of plenty,
And whether I see her stooping, or leaning with the flowers,
What she does is ages old, and she is not simply,
No, but lovely in that way.

A Defence of Breathing

Michael Donaghy on the new formality among American women poets

A Formal Feeling Comes,
edited by Annie Finch,
Story Line Press $15.75, ISBN 0 934257 98 1
Marilyn Hacker,
Selected Poems 1965-1990,
WW Norton, $22, ISBN 0 393 03675 8
Winter Numbers,
WW Norton $17.95 ISBN 0 393 03674 X

A *Formal Feeling Comes* has got to be the worst anthology title since *The New Naked Poetry*. It's Dickinson ('After great pain, a formal feeling comes – '), but that's no excuse. That poem is about grief and continues: 'The Feet mechanical, go round –/ Of Ground, or Air, or Ought/ A Wooden way'./which is the last thing you want to hear about anyone's poetry. Title aside, this is a milestone, the first anthology to document the widespread return to formal poetics among American women poets.

The editor, Annie Finch, has selected sixty one poets, among them Marilyn Hacker, Carolyn Kizer, Rachel Hadas, Mary Jo Salter, and Rita Dove, the current American laureate. For some reason undoubtedly beyond Finch's control, one of the best American formalists, Gertrude Schnackenburg, is missing (on the plus side, I discovered Finch's own work.)

The poems range from sapphics to sestinas, the personal to the geopolitical, the elegy to the phillipic, from Kizer's exuberance in 'Pro Femina' to Rhina Espalillat's deceptive modesty in 'Metrics':

> All things, however magneted by cause,
> Should bear their nature's imprint to the end;
> Should shadow forth the whole to which they tend,
> But keep small laws.

And all the poets provide introductory remarks on their own practice. There are one or two antimodernist zealots among them, but mostly they defend their right to reclaim the formal option and their lineage in an American tradition that includes Sara Teasdale, Alice Dunbar Nelson, Edna Millay, Elinor Wylie, and Charlotte Mew.

Did you wince at the mention of those names? Even if you've never read them? Modernist critics did their worst to make them synonymous with sentimentality and technical obsolescence in an era when Pound dictated 'poetry speaks phallic direction', and by mid-century all had either fallen out of print or been dropped by anthologists. Nevertheless, their accessible, traditional, and often politically radical verse enjoyed a considerable readership during the first decades of the century. According to the poets included here, the long exile is over.

In claiming this heritage, the poets in Finch's anthology express what they feel is a uniquely female approach to form. Several follow Louise Bogan's lead and argue the case from nature – the heart's iamb. 'Writing about the iambic pentameter', says Carolyn Kizer, 'is like writing a defence of breathing'. Molly Peacock and Mary Kinzie liken formal practice to traditional 'feminine' crafts: weaving, quilting and embroidery.

But the most intriguing difference is their surrender to what used to be called the Muse. Contemporary male poets and critics tend to view formalism in terms of 'authority', 'mastery' – the impress of the will on language. The poets in this anthology are more interested in serendipity, the rewards of negotiating with the demands of rhyme and metre. Kelly Cherry finds traditional forms 'like maps of places no one's ever been. They lead the writer into uncharted territory'. For Phyllis Levin, 'embracing form is a form of embracing fate, of simultaneously accepting and resisting, absorbing and shaping the forces of language and life, the interplay of the arbitrary and the given with the shaped and the chosen'. Maura Stanton speaks of a deeper force 'shaping my lines and giving me a mysterious new entry into my imagination'. 'Meter', says editor Finch, 'led me into – and out, of my own labyrinths ... communion with form can distract me, so that the poem comes out by itself'.

Marilyn Hacker is the most frequently cited contemporary influence in *A Formal Feeling Comes.* But you won't find her in the *Dictionary of Literary Biography*, or in Helen Vendler's anthology of *Contemporary American Poetry*, or even in Gibert and Gubar's *Norton Anthology of Literature by Women.* In spite of her five volumes and more than twenty-five years' work as poet and editor, she's only recently been granted the attention she deserves. Perhaps critics find it difficult to categorize her. Like Adrienne Rich, she writes a poetry of engagement, of lesbian feminist politics and the politics of the personal. But where Rich abandoned received forms with *Diving Into The Wreck,* Hacker, from the start of her career, has embraced them with gusto.

She's done them all, like a compulsive collector. Her *Selected Poems 1965-1990* features hendecasyllabics, rondeau redoublé, ballades, canzones, crowns of sonnets, pantoums, sapphics. There are so many sestinas in this book I felt relieved every time I found I wasn't reading one. This doesn't square comfortably with poets like Carole Oles, who does her best to make Hacker more acceptable in her essay 'The Feminist Literary Movement': 'Tension between the direct, woman-centered content of (Hacker's) poems and the patriarchal, canonical forms constitutes a reappropriation'. You can tell from her tone she really doesn't approve of all that showing off.

Hacker, she says, uses form subversively. But in fact, she uses it for the perfectly ordinary business of argument, seduction, elegy, and celebration. It's her content that's subversive, and all the more effectively so for the care she takes to make it memorable.

In a ballade, 'Graffiti from the Gare Saint-Manque' she admonishes feminists who eschew reason and form and seek salvation exclusively in 'the Female subconscious':

> Suspiciously like Girlish Ignorance,
> it seems a rather watery solution.
> If I can't dance, it's not any revolution.
> If I can't think about it, I won't dance.
> So let the ranks of *Psyche et Po* include
> another Jewish Lesbian in France.

– that last line being the poems refrain. This isn't rhyme of the concealed, subliminal, or at least discreet variety, but the outrageous neo-Byronic sort that trumpets even its failures. You can no more forget that Hacker is rhyming than you can forget that the characters in *La Bohème* are singing. She enjambs with no regard for the voice, finds end rhymes in the middles of words, and habitually rhymes French words with English.

Some of these poems are verse epistles dedicated to her daughter, Iva, or to lovers, or to other poets – and here the elaborate craft is a demonstration of love, like the careful selection of food and drink that features prominently throughout the latter half of this volume. Others chronicle, without self-pity, the events of her difficult life; a *menage à trois,* the death of a young lover, and her alienation among the lunatics and junkies of New York and San Francisco – and here the form functions as it did for the young Adrienne Rich, like asbestos gloves enabling her to handle and express the grief, rage, fear and loss.

There are dramatic monologues (a letter from Harriet Tubman to Amelia Bloomer ordering her eponymous garment) and a 'Ballad of Ladies Lost and Found', with its refrain 'and plain old Margaret Fuller died as well' (a variation on Villon's *'Ou Sont Les Neiges D'Antan').* It's a triumphant roll call of remarkable literary women, gay or straight, forgotten or misremembered. One of the most moving poems is dedicated to the poet's ex-mother-in-law, Margaret Delany, 'Black working poor, unduped, and civilized', now silenced by a stroke

> A hemisphere
> away from understanding where you are,
> mourning your lost words, I am at a loss
> for words to name what my loss of you is,
> what it will be, or even what it was.

Winter Numbers contains her best work to date: tributes to friends lost to AIDS, a chronicle of her own fight against breast cancer. The 'numbers' of the title refer to the archaic term for verse, but also to mortality statistics 'one in nine, one in three' and to the ages of her dying friends: 'The bookseller who died at thirty nine/ poet at fifty eight, friend, fifty one,/ friend, fifty five. These numbers do not sing'. Throughout she weighs these personal losses against the enormity of the Holocaust and questions her right to reduce their lives to poetry: 'I can only bear witness for my own/ dead and dying'.

Occasionally Hacker allows the form to push her lines into something like cryptic crossword clues, and some of the poems seem to get lost in waffle halfway through, as if the form had mugged the poet and grabbed the wheel. When that happens we're taken on a long drive through picturesque countryside including a stop for lunch. I suppose this is part of her method. As she says in 'Corona'–

> Considered as just measures for a line,
> sound more than sense determines words I choose
> invention mutes intention. If the shoes
> you bought were grey suede clogs size thirty-nine
> if we sang passions matins and compline
> I'm storytelling....

– because, as she reveals, 'They're brown, your oxfords, and size forty one'. I advise you to sit back and enjoy the ride. Her best work profits from this playfulness. Besides, it's a mark of good sense that she finds the world full of more serious things than verse, and this makes even her wittiest verse profoundly serious.

ALICE FRIMAN
Letter to the Children

In the new cold of late September
the prongs of Queen Anne's lace that held
its doily up like a jewel
rise then stiffen, crushing toward center,
making a wooden enclosure to die in
like the ones the Celts built to hold their enemies
then set aflame. The goldenrod leans,
licks at their cages. And all that's left of daisies
are burnt out eyes.

I walk these back fields
past the swish of cattail in their silver
grasses, the old ones
showing the woolly lining of their suede jackets,
while the thistle, dried to gray,
bends her trembling head
and spills her seed.

It is the time – the great lying-in of Autumn –
and I am walking its wards.
And I remember it was now, late September
then on into the deep gully of fall – when the hackberry
groans and the black oak strains in its sockets, the winds
pushing in the long forest corridors –
that I too was born and gave birth.

And you are all Autumn's children, all
given to sadness amid great stirrings
for you were rocked to sleep in the knowledge
of loss and saw in the reflection outside your window,
beyond the bars of your reach, your own face
beckoning from the burning promise
that little by little disappeared. What can I give you
for your birthdays this year, you who are the match
and the flaming jewel, whose birthright consumes itself
in the face of your desire?

If you were here with me now
walking down this day's death,
I would try to show you two things: how the last light
plays itself out over the thistle's labors,
over the wild cherry heavy with fruit, as if comfort
lay in what it had made. And how that black bird
with flame at his shoulders
teeters for balance on a swaying weed.

Alice Friman has published 5 collections in the USA, the latest being* Driving for Jimmy Wonderland *(Barnwood).

Vibrating Strings

by Martyn Crucefix

David Harsent,
Newsfrom the Front,
OUP, £7.99,
ISBN 019 2831038
Storybook Hero,
Sycamore Press, 4 Benson Place,
Oxford OX2 6QH, £3.00

The last poem in the strange and ambitious book-length sequence, *News from the Front*, records an interesting effect: 'A slammed door sings / in the strings of the upright grand'. As the metaphor of the Aeolian harp helped to characterize the inspiration and verse of the Romantics, perhaps Harsent has given us here an image for some of the most interesting poetry of our time. Certainly, it serves to elucidate this book which contains the kind of poetry I ought to like. It comes complete with a prefatory Argument suggesting how much the sequence owes to a specific narrative situation worked out in detail and at length (80 pages), and goes on to indicate that the 'imaginings' of the characters cut firmly through their 'reality'.

The story is that a man goes to war, leaving behind his pregnant common-law wife. A boy is born. The man writes letters home and keeps a journal (which includes a Bestiary for the boy). The woman lives close to Dartmoor, seeing 'visions' of the absent father. The boy falls in with this, transforming the man into a hero. Harsent says that he makes 'free use' of this 'drama of separation'. Quite frankly, I found the use made of the situation bewilderingly free and I doubt whether I would have grasped what was going on if it had not been for the Argument. The same last poem in the book talks of 'this almost-/ random collage of re-written letters, / of photos, of squibs / /and quips noted down / in a kind of code'. The self-deprecating tone aside (there is never a moment when Harsent doubts the significance of the poems), this is a far better description of the impact of the sequence than talk of a 'drama of separation'. There is really very little drama as such, since there is only the most sketchy of characterization. What we do have is a clear initial slam of the door – 'with her back to the wall / and the Devil to pay / she got up on her toes / for the boy in the red beret'. The implications of this event are then played out biologically in the birth of the child, emotionally in the three characters, repeated turnings to each other throughout the next several years, and poetically in the sustained chiming of individual strings – letters, photos, squibs, quips – in other words, the poems themselves. The result, as with the slam-responding piano, is a single chord which, though dissonant, is struck out of the diversity. Without devolving authority to any one discourse (character or viewpoint), this writing gives the reader a sense of a whole, suggesting that the evaluation (and so the meaning) of experience arises out of such interrelations. The Bestiary that the soldier writes for his son takes its meaning and power from the ironic contrast between its intended audience and the actuality of battlefield life: 'The dog is a big itch. / You don't have to get close / to see his ears are swarming with mites // or the cherry sores, / big as your fist, / that he digs his hindpaw into'.

This, as it were, alignment of dissonances can give rise to the most exciting poetry. It can also become an easy stylistic habit and sometimes it is not clear what ultimate use Harsent wants to make of his 'drama of separation'. Both the man's and woman's world are vividly conceived – though the man's trench-life has a (perhaps) inevitable familiarity to it. The woman's life, crisscrossed with domesticity, pagan relics and beliefs and the natural world of Dartmoor offers some of the best passage in the book: 'She was as lonely / as a woman with two husbands / ... driftless, no more than a guest / like the rafter's pipistrelle / or the toad, stock-still beside the flour-keg, / stunned by its diamond solitaire'.

Another high point is the section 'Storybook Hero' in which the growing boy hero-worships the father: 'When they were done / they rolled him off the tailgate, // dappled with lilac and lemon / bruises and wiser than ever'. The full complexity of the reading experience here was not evident when this part of the whole appeared as a limited edition pamphlet from John Fuller's Sycamore Press. What was missing were the vibrating strings either side of it – the actual father's unheroic voice ('Each battle / winnows me from myself') and the mother's powerful presence ('He wanted to loaf / under the skirt of her coat all winter'). It is only in these longer, echoey perspectives that the richness of such writing truly emerges. This, in the end, is the real significance of Harsent's use of his characters' 'imaginings'. They are not daydreams, but expressions of desire and belief as powerful – and this is surely the point of the contrast – as powerful as the trench-life of the absent father: 'A boot under the shoulder turns one of them up, his face / foaming with worms'.

The Stone Stony

by Robert Crawford

Iain Crichton Smith,
Collected Poems,
Carcanet £25
ISBN 085635 956 4
Ends and Beginnings,
Carcanet, £8.95
ISBN 1 85754 093 X

Though Iain Crichton Smith published his first collection in the 1950s, the bulk of his work has appeared in the last two decades. It was part of the Scottish literary climate I grew up in, and I find it hard to distance myself from it. When I do stand back, I find what I like best are not necessarily Smith's best-known poems. Powerful though they are, his many accounts of determined old women trapped by circumstance, or of religious or educational strictness insinuate their way into my consciousness less sinuously than harder to classify short poems. Here, for instance, is the whole of 'Owl and Mouse':

> The owl wafts home with a mouse in its beak.
> The moon is stunningly bright in the high sky.
>
> Such a gold stone, such a brilliant hard light.
> Such large round eyes of the owl among the trees.
>
> All seems immortal but for the dangling mouse,
> an old hurt string among the harmony
>
> of the masterful and jewelled orchestra
> which shows no waste soundlessly playing on.

This finely-cut poem may deal sensitively with the theme of remorselessness common in the work of this one-time schoolteacher, born on Lewis in 1928. What impresses me not least is the way it does so in clear images without preaching. Smith's gift for images and telling phrases is evident on almost any page of his work, but sometimes there is a wordiness or moralizing that, through trying to intensify it, softens the poems' blow.

Smith has always been attracted to long poems or sequences, and scored a notable success early in his career with 'Deer on the High Hills', a poem that tries to fuse the forbidding sense of the inhuman in MacDiarmid's 'On a Raised Beach' with the more loving attention paid to nature by the Gaelic master Duncan Ban Macintyre, whose 'Ben Dorain' Smith later translated. I'm never sure how much I like the most quoted lines from 'Deer on the High Hills', which speak of how 'the stone is stony and the sun is sunny, / the deer step out in isolated air', but they do haunt me. There is probably too much casing round that poem's core, though; it's longer than it needs to be. Smith's later sequences such as *The Village* tend to group poems in little communities, where images in one poem visit those in another without quite repeating them. Always he has an eye for stringent loveliness. His enemy is the wordy Muse of Education.

Much of Smith's best work has a bare quality that often involves reaching down below the level of the teacher's explanatory rhetoric and is frequently bound up with the Gaelic-speaking world he comes from. A bilingual poet, he frequently translates into English from his own Gaelic. The small prose pieces in *The Permanent Island* (1975) have a powerful flavour that verges on translatorese and, at their finest, have an oracular brevity. Here is the poem 'Bareness' : 'It is bareness I want, the bareness of the knife's blade. And the words to be going away from me like ducks settling on the sea when night is falling, their wings folded on the sea, and the night falling'. Other work by Smith is easier to paraphrase, but the self-contained quality of this has a resisting dignity that's hard to beat or explain. A similar resisting dignity, an obstinacy born from another way of life, is present in the wonderful sequence of poetic pebbles, 'Gaelic Stories', which brings the haiku into Gaelic, then translates that Gaelic into a straight-faced English that will always make me smile:

> A conversation
> between fresh butter
> and a cup.

This, in context, is part of a great humorous and serious poem about the isolated way of life of the Hebrides, time hanging heavy in domestic interiors. The poem's vignettes grow a culture around them, like some potent poetic virus. This is one of Smith's finest works, inexplicably absent from his *Collected Poems,* which makes one wonder about the editing of those.

This worry persists when I read the new collection *Ends & Beginnings,* a book riven with beauty, but also uneven. The attractive lines, 'It is time to turn the blow lamp on dogma/ and inhabit this blue', end the poem 'As Time Draws Near'; the same lines end the poem 'A Day without Dogma'. In 'Aberdeen' the poet tells us 'I used to shout out lines from *Othello*/ as I passed the cemeteries// Put up your bright swords or the dew will rust them'; in the poem 'In Aberdeen' we're told 'I walked by the cemetery/ reciting from *Othello*// 'Put up your bright swords/ or the dew will rust them.' Smith tends to rewrite certain poems obsessively, but it is surely a flaw to make this so obvious. A more thorough edit would have left a book in tune with Smith's strongest, pithiest poems. Yet this is a collection rich in good writing, often on topics it is hard to write well about. A poem on a favourite cat recalls that 'The icy Bible says/that an animal has no soul', and ends 'I see you flying,/our miniature lion,/permanently alone'. Again, as in Smith's other, very different successes there is a triumph of dignity over sentiment that enhances rather than loses emotional impact. Smith is one of our most consistently enjoyable poets. To read him is not only to experience an indvidual sensibility but to gain access to a culture which articulates through him a sense of community, humour, bleakness and wiry dignity. Few, once they read it, fail to return to his work.

E.A. MARKHAM
A Philpot & A Wife

There is no other identification on his body.
Not dead, they taunt the wife who isn't his.
She comes to hospital to pronounce him alien
to class and race: that portrait is not of family.

Her husband, the doctor, wears no uniform,
has never thrown her down the stairs (wrong house)
nor, in the shower, helped anyone to slip on soap:
she must stay sane, despite the change in life.

Another deep breath, the children are off her hands
to conjure daemons. So to her challenge
from the wrong side of town, a Philpot without family,
the size of guilt; protector. There may be worse to come.

She sees him pummelled, a presence in the garden,
a '60s throwback, a Pinter matchseller. Could it be
her lover stuck for words? But women here are spoken for.
At best someone will use Philpot to shore the losing

argument. So give him four lines to say his piece.
Stripped of nonsense he can't fill them, but mumbles
something of a daughter who has problems with her kidneys,
and of Herr Doktor, uniformed, wifed, who caused it.

E. A. Markham's latest collection is* Letter from Ulster & The Hugo Poems *(Littlewood Arc, 1993)

The Late Word

by Anthony Rudolf

Carolyn Forché,
The Angel of History,
Bloodaxe Books, £7.95
ISBN 1 85224 307 4

'The spiritual authenticity of a charred journal extracted from rubble, one written in secret by a poet whose name we do not know ... Tsvetayeva? Pauline Celan?' Derek Walcott's unfortunate gender recuperation of the greatest poet of the Holocaust strikes a false note in his otherwise eloquent and moving back-cover homage to this important and difficult book and its author. Caroline Forché is a strong enough poet not to need straitjacketing. Her sequence of poems incarnates a non-linear process of remembrance, a fragmentary meditation owing something to Pound, even more to another great poet, one who confronted Pound head-on and heart-on, George Oppen: 'If we died we might escape the sovereignty of the accidental'. In syntax and measure, Forché treads carefully and deliberately through this Adorno-challenged minefield.

Her subject is war and, yes, the pity of it: the Shoah, the Bomb and the Gulag – surely the matrix-events of the twentieth century – and, in their shadow, the later wars we who come after have failed to prevent, slouching as we are towards our universal ignominy. The pressure of history on experience, wrote Milosz. Here Forché generates a poetic discourse quite explicitly from history, literature and experience – the psychogeometry of her own experience and the experiential modalities of those on the receiving end of the worst that history, i.e.individuals making a choice, has thrown at its children – a discourse re-presenting, mirroring that eternal triangle of forces, that three-fold matrix. ('Figures dead and alive/whispering not truth but a need for truth when one word is many things').

Forché's text is a verbal mobile, deploying in the main a long line, a *verset*. It is, quite rightly, an anxious book, opening and closing with celebrated extracts from Walter Benjamin and Paul Valéry. Forché is no peasant ploughing on while Icarus falls into the sea. The field is a minefield. Does she have the right to make a thing of beauty – for that is what her book is – when children are dying in the killing fields of El Salvador and elsewhere? This is a proper question and she, in effect, asks it of herself. If I am to incarnate grief in words chosen for maximum effect and affect of sense/sound (thus, one among many: 'as long as it takes snow to slip from the snow piles/a memory barely retrieved from a fire is the past in its hiding place') – her book seems to say – I must build into the manner of my saying an awareness of my fragility and the risk I am taking.

Like another of her tutelary presences, Claude Lanzmann ('a swastika on rue Boulard'), Forché brings the dead to our attention so that we shall die with them in our solitary reading, when briefly they are not alone. ('What was here before imperfectly erased/and memory a reliquary in a wall of silence'). Fifty years after the liberation of Auschwitz, the poet who dares to enter this domain cannot, even if she wanted to, write in an unmediated way. Like it or not, the writing has to be a reading. Celan and Levi have already been there. Lanzmann and Martin Gilbert have already been there. Rawicz and Antelme have already been there. A new historicism, as James Young insists, is right and proper.

Forché's book is a 'station of reading in the late word', to quote Paul Celan. She appropriates in an appropriate way. Ambition in this minefield demands modesty. 'What use are poets in hard times?', asked Hölderlin. The answer is: to serve as witness that private and public expressions of language can respect and even honour each other's necessity. This is the only politics available to the poet *qua* poet. *Qua* citizen? Ah, that is another story. When the messiah shall come and the language of the *polis* shall be redeemed, poetry will be out of a job. Meanwhile, there is work to do.

The Suffering is Elsewhere

by Dennis O'Driscoll

Harry Smart,
Shoah,
Faber, £5.99
ISBN 0 571 16793 4
Fool's Pardon,
Faber, £6.99
ISBN 0 571 17359 4

Harry Smart's books line up nose-to-tail like planes ready for take-off, *Shoah* and *Fool's Pardon* swiftly following his 1991 debut, *Pierrot*. It would require a rare talent to publish a worthwhile collection so often and an even rarer one to alchemise the more banal elements of his work into poetry. The first poem in *Shoah*, for instance, which records a flight from Gatwick to Berlin, serves up some real stodge; a return flight to England provides an even bumpier ride for the reader:

From up here, I can tell you,
the cloud looks terrific, un-
symbolic, and I feel damn fine.
In Club Europe class I've just been
served wine, smoked salmon, veal, and

feine Trüffel-Praline from Rausch.
I'm sipping my Drambuie
and I feel damn fine. Someone else
is paying. The suffering is elsewhere ...

'The suffering is elsewhere' assures us that, complimentary Drambuies notwithstanding, our poet has not forgotten his moral baggage. His head may be in the 'un-symbolic' clouds but his heart is in the right place. However, despite allusions to the Olympic murders of 1972 and the killing of a Gastarbeiter, the opening German sequence amounts to little more than holiday jottings: 'Rain fell. I checked the map' or 'We shopped for music,/ listened to Sam Cooke singing 'Wonderful World',/ then slept'. Some poems burst abruptly into German, like an exercise in poetic pentecostalism. If the centrepiece of *Shoah*, six poems by Rainer Malkowski, can be translated from the German, why can't Smart's own poetry?

The title-sequence of *Shoah* is a retelling of the Flood story from Genesis by reference to the Jewish Holocaust. Big themes do not, of course, guarantee great poems any more than the gratuitous insertion of swastikas and chimneys in certain paintings automatically confers a higher significance on them. 'What can poetry do against a wall/Of skulls?', Smart had asked in his first collection; his response in *Shoah* is full of earnestness and ominousness but fatally lacking in resonance. His language, while appropriately austere, never manages to suggest – let alone convey – the awful reality which Holocaust diaries, letters, chronicles and memoirs so harrowingly adumbrate. The sequence (indebted both to Ted Hughes and Claude Lanzmann) fails to touch that core of silence which its ineffable theme demands. Spare though the poems are, the effect is oddly garrulous: Smart's ark is an empty vessel making hollow sounds.

With a few honourable exceptions (such as 'The Don'), Smart's less public poems in his latest offering, *Fool's Pardon*, are aimless, inconsequential and occasionally downright embarrassing: 'Sitting in bed, Catriona and I had finished our Frosties,/Ben, aged three, had almost finished his ... '. On the political front the results are no better: the Ulster situation is one about which 'no-one is qualified to speak, or everyone is' (an insight paralleled in the macaronic 'Zu Hause', which concludes that 'language is the only thing belongs/to no-one and to everyone'). Then there is 'The Leader', combining free association with a free German lesson ('Hitler flog. Flog Hitler. Hitler flew, irregular verb/in German as in English',) and the equally risible 'After Bosnia' in which Smart adopts a regular form and a superior tone:

Yet more *plus ça change*
Yet more slender means.
Yet more artistic integrity.
Yet more hill of beans.

For this is British poetry,
and isn't it fine:
total moral bankruptcy
and a pure poetic line.

Personally, I would trade a 'pure poetic line' for the cluttered thinking of *Fool's Pardon*. One bizarre poem, occasioned – or, rather, provoked – by the unveiling of a statue to Arthur 'Bomber' Harris in 1992, was apparently first written in German because 'I can't write it /in English. To be English is/ almost unbearable'. If unwarranted bombing is the issue, I am puzzled as to how German can be the solution; at any rate, this crude poem *is* printed both in German and English. According to a note in a recent issue of *Stand*, 'The original of this poem, in German, was offered to the BBC's *The Late Show*. The offer was, naturally, not acknowledged'. Maybe the poem has lost something in translation; judged by the English version, however, the reaction of *The Late Show* was indeed a 'natural' one:

To be a piece of flesh is very dangerous.
I'm just a piece of flesh, and today, here,
to be a piece of English flesh is unbearable.
Today, to write about the Holocaust in English
is simply not in very good taste.

IAN GREGSON

Natural Heir

'Natural heir of Eliot and Auden . . .

scholarship and street cred.
Inner city, house and garden,
beautifully written ... in bed.
House parent and wildlife warden.'

'. . . monster, honest. Fiction-making.
Honest ventriloquist.
Doing voices and police. Piss-taking.
Self-reflexively pissed.'

'Blurb surreally infiltrated.
Hard poet seeking same, and discipline.
Different registers mated.
Travels vast distance in a line.'

'. . .'

'Flickering catwalks, subways, smashed booths,
Underbelly starkly revealed.
Ludic surgeon, magic home truths.
. . . fingers in the scherzo most appealed.'
'He lives in Huddersfield.'

'One of the most athletic post-war singers.
Quirky, alert. Propulsion. Dread.
Muscular . . . articulate fingers.
Massive authority in bed.'

'Witty flavour, moving gravy. *Do me a favour,*
tell your husband way with language.
Nous, sweetheart, and a tauter, braver,
bacon, lettuce and tomato sandwich.'

'Tight rhymes and two great feet.
Hunkily dangerous demeanour.
Biting, savage. What a way to treat
A ballerina!'

REVIEWS

The Phantom Rider

Michael Hulse on an addition to the modern pantheon of long poems

David Constantine,
Caspar Hauser,
Bloodaxe 6.95
ISBN 1 85224 299 X

Fourteen years ago I visited Ansbach and went to see the stone that marks the spot where Caspar Hauser was knifed, in the gardens of the Orangery, in 1833. It was mid-December when he was killed. Snow was on the ground. He dragged himself home across town and took three days to die. Someone told me that, in German, Caspar Hauser was the second most written-about person in history – the first, interestingly, not being Hitler but Napoleon. I have never checked this, but there is certainly a vast literature on Hauser, and the fact that one feels it might just be true is itself revealing.

Briefly, the story is this. On Whit Monday 1829, a curiously-dressed youth who could say only one sentence, 'I want to be a rider like my father', appeared out of nowhere in Nuremberg. It emerged that he had been kept from infancy in close confinement, and as a result he was entirely ignorant of the sights, sounds, scents and tastes that now assailed him, and was enchanted and terrified by turns. His senses responded with extraordinary keenness: 'He could tell apple, pear and plum trees apart at a distance of over a hundred paces by the smell of their leaves', wrote Anselm von Feuerbach, the criminologist, while another witness reported: 'Out walking at dusk, he made out the black berries on an elder tree at a distance of about a hundred and fifty yards and described the way in which they differed from blackberries, with which he was already familiar'. Speculation as to his identity was rife, and the processes by which he acquired language and skills, and lost his special sensitivities, were monitored with the avidity so characteristic of the 19th century. Feuerbach reached a conclusion that many have since agreed with, that Hauser was in fact the lost first son of Grand Duchess Stephanie of Baden, the adopted daughter and protegée of Napoleon. Whatever the truth, at least one attempt was made on his life before he was murdered in Ansbach. The writers and artists have always loved him: Verlaine, Rilke and Trakl wrote poems, Jakob Wassermann wrote the best of many novels, Peter Handke wrote a play, Werner Herzog made a film, and Suzanne Vega wrote a song about Caspar Hauser (on her second album).

David Constantine's treatment, in nine cantos arranged in partially rhymed tercets of irregular metre (though with a recurring, muscular up-twist into the iambic), is an important poem, alert and sensitive, the best thing he has written to date. Three framing cantos enclose six flashbacks in which principals in the story, near their own deaths, recall their relations with Caspar. At the outset, Constantine has exactly the right words to show how out of things his subject is:

> [...] time for Caspar was as Luther guessed
> It might be for God: all in a heap, at rest.

Constantine gives little attention to the issues that have preoccupied German writers – language, cognition, the relation of sense evidence to these– but nonetheless packs large implication into a single image: 'He felt like ants in a stabbed and burgled hill'. I don't think I have seen the milling, despoiled, bewildered condition of Caspar in the early days put better.

Daumer, the teacher who was Caspar's first guardian, gets three cantos. He watches Caspar change: 'the light went off him as off a landed rainbow trout'. He monitors 'the more or less of sadness'. After the first attempt on Caspar's life, Daumer sits down with a razor: 'Why not draw a thin red smile with it from ear to ear?' But he doesn`t. Daumer is dry, obsessive, pathetic. To Clara Biberbach, the lady of Caspar's next household, Constantine gives one canto, indulgently tracing her history of marital frustration, of longing to be 'Masked and naked in a *maison de passe* / For a couple of captains'. She and 'her shivery image in the glass' agree that it will be okay to dress and undress in front of Caspar, as ladies do before their black attendants; but Caspar's innocent member never stirs (she checks). Two cantos go to the most elusive figure in the tale, Philip Henry, Earl Stanhope, the English lord who took so ambivalent an interest in Caspar Hauser. The great debating point to this day is whether Stanhope was acting for third parties who wanted Hauser dead, and arranged the killing; rumour has it that the Stanhope family still refuse to show historians papers in their possession. David Constantine seems to want it both ways, finding in Stanhope a passion to do the Lord's work but stressing his knowledge that the snow in Ansbach:

Was red for all to see
With scribbles nobody could understand but
me.

At a time when (despite Walcott, Merrill, Ondaatje, Murray, Curnow, Heaney and many more) we're often told that the long poem is dead, David Constantine's *Caspar Hauser* joins Craig Raine's *History* and Paul Muldoon's 'Yarrow' (in *The Annals of Chile*) as yet another reminder that it can still go the distance. Even so, ironically, the poem's finest, utterly moving moment comes in the eighth canto, when Constantine steps aside from his narrative, into the present, to think of the outsiders in our midst now, the ones we so rarely communicate with. In a passage that seems to come from a lyrical meditation rather than an epic, he describes being buttonholed by a beggar in the Tube, made to listen to 'the whine of the last trains', their 'ghostly doubling in the underground winds', sounds 'like falling through eternity'– and then going on, thinking 'I should have had him home'. He concludes this canto, with a bare force such as rarely comes off (but here it does):

He would be still there if I ever went that way.
I don't. He frightens me.

Best never look. I hear the scream
Most nights. I see his bit of card: to whom

It may concern. I read my name.

Michael Hulse translated Jakob Wassermann's **Caspar Hauser** ***for Penguin Twentieth Centry Classics.***

ATAR HADARI

Doctor

When you are done with your killing
and curing – when all the arms are set –
ligaments re-knitted, shins straight,
hip-joints freely hinged to rotate
why – when the last face is powdered,
last curler set into heat and last corpse gone home
will you have lived? You put off the master
– when death comes, will they come to *your* bed
to put him off? And lined, shuffling to transfer
their lives like grains of white sugar will one good cup
of black coffee strong as the mixture in our veins
be sweetened? Will one soul helped
name you as you face your maker
or will you look out
at the roses bloomed from the grass
in amongst all the blue tombstones –
will you have had a life
when all those you have saved have passed?
And the breadcrumbs. The wet in your mouth
the last soft clothes you put away
will they call you from the hamper
and say 'we'd have let you win
but you never played'?
And my stories – carved on the ice-cubes
that float to the river's open weir
they are no sop to disaster
but they'll stand a wall round my bed
when my soul's thief desires to leave.

Atar Hadari's verse plays have been staged by Derek Walcott's Boston Playwrights' Theatre.

Fit for Heroes

by John Bayley

Christopher Logue,
The Husbands,
Faber, £6.99
ISBN 0 571 17198 2

To the ancient world Homer was the vatic genius and lord of language who had, as we say, established the guidelines. Greek heroic society lived by him and through him: he was at once exemplar and ideal. He was the great exponent of what much later came to be known rather pompously as the Tragic View of Life: though to the Greeks there was nothing particularly tragic about it – it was just life. But superlife of course. The great Achilles was Alexander the Great's conscious model: the invincible warrior whose final achievement is heroic failure. Heroes need above all to be remembered, to have their deeds recorded. When Hannibal, a barbarian hero but a completely Hellenized one, set out to cross the Alps, he took a couple of Greek historians with him to make sure that what he did would not be forgotten.

To make it live again is rather different. It takes a poet like Christopher Logue, in whose language the old ideal can be seen almost visibly working, to give us through language the sort of thrills that Homer gave. In the *Iliad* these are physical, indeed visceral. What does it feel like to get your spear under the bronze and into the belly of your opponent? What does it feel like to have it done to you? Poetry can tell us, and in *The Husbands*, as in his two previous Homeric home movies, Christopher Logue does it incomparably well.

Indeed I think *The Husbands* is superior in this respect even to *War Music* and *Kings*, superlative as their action poetry was. Homer's language can be – indeed for much of the time is – calm, tranquil and foreboding: Dawn with her rose fingers seems to know there is about to be an explosion, but her coming is all the more serene in consequence. One of the most Homeric comments in Shakespeare's game with the ancient poet, in *Troilus and Cressida*, is that of Ulysses:

> Time hath, my Lord, a wallet on his back
> Wherein he puts alms for oblivion.

Much of Logue's speech in *The Husbands* (who are Menelaos the Spartan king from whom Helen has been stolen, and Paris the thief) is in the same calmly sinister vein.

And remarkably effective it is. How about the moment when Pandarus with his bow is about to take a crafty shot at Menelaos, as he throws back his head to drain a cup of wine?

> And, as his chin goes up, child Pandar
> sights his throat
> Then frees the nock, and gently as the
> snow
> Falls from an ilex leaf on to the snow
> Athene left him, and the head moved out.

Even at its most cryptic the style never tries to be 'beautiful'. There is even something faintly derisive about it; and this effect, though not Homeric in itself, is the modern equivalent of the heroic style, though genuinely full-blooded. ('Child', incidentally, is the old English term for hero or knight, as in Child Harold and Child Roland: while the third in line in the quote is purely Tennysonian. Logue's omnivorous scholarship is richly unobtrusive.)

Athene leaves her favourite, Menelaos, but even as she leaves she tips the arrow down so that it hits him not in the throat but in the 'pubic mound', painfully but not terminally. Paris's guardian Aphrodite had similarly intervened in the single combat between her favourite and Menelaos. The Spartan king had felled his opponent and was about to give the *coup de grace* when his sword flew to bits on Paris's helmet.

> No problem!
> A hundred of us pitch our swords to him
> ...
> Yet even as they flew, their blades
> Changed into wings, their pommels into
> heads,
> Their hilts to feathered chests, and what
> were swords
> Were turned to doves, a swirl of doves,
> And waltzing up to it, in oyster silk,
> Running her tongue around her strawberry
> lips
> While repositioning a spaghetti shoulder-
> strap,
> The Queen of Love, our Lady Aphrodite,
> Touching the massive Greek aside with
> one
> Pink finger-tip, and with her other hand
> Lifting Lord Paris up, lacing his fingers
> with her own,
> The leading him, hidden in wings, away.

This is the perfect modern equivalent of Homer's sense of touch and gesture, movement and position. A goddess, like a girl, puts her tongue a little out as she settles a delinquent ribbon; a goddess can also push a brawny hero out of her way with one finger.

Satisfying as it is to read this wonderful stuff on the page, I think it really requires a skilled elocutionist in the Homeric style to do it justice. The movement of the verse, choppy and turbulent, but also full of its own underlying rhythm, changing and returning like wave patterning, needs to be smoothed into acoustic coherence so that the ear can instantly take it in. James Fenton reads many of his poems very well this way; I don't know if Logue does, but most poets read badly, perhaps from a sense that all their labour has gone into composition, and someone else must master the almost equally tricky art of reciting it. Perhaps Homer too felt like that, but his poetry was written – or rather composed – to be read; and Logue's verse too deserves fluent and accomplished acting out.

'An inch beneath Homer's sunlit surface is hell', said C. S. Lewis; contrapuntally, Shakespeare is imagining something not so different in *Troilus and Cressida*. In its own comprehensive way, as it speaks of 'hateful Ares', the god of war, and of the futile struggles and sufferings of men besieging and defending a city, the *Iliad* itself bears witness to this obvious truth. And yet war is itself the great object of life and manhood, the great football game, and Logue's poem underlines with admirable vigour this message and moral of heroic poetry, its acceptance of its own desolation. 'And you too, old man, were, as we have heard, once happy', as Achilles says to the grieving Priam. 'Joy after wo, and wo after gladnesse', as Chaucer puts it in *The Knight's Tale*. There is nothing tender-hearted about such poetry, except by the bleakest sort of implication: this suits Logue's idiom, as probably that of much other brilliant contemporary verse. The end of his poem (which let us hope will be continued indefinitely) is on a wholly appropriate note of anti-climax, with the rumble of the guns dying away, as they do at the end of Britten's *War Requiem* and Wilfred Owen's 'Strange Meeting'. But in Homer, as in Logue, nothing is here for tears.

> And now it has passed us the sound of their war
> Resembles the sound of Niagara
> Heard from afar in the still of the night.

Les Murray Advises Anger

by Laurie Smith

Peter Porter,
Millennial Fables,
Oxford University Press,
£7.99, ISBN 0 19 282391 4

In his essay 'On Sitting Back and Thinking About Porter's Boeotia', the Australian poet Les Murray defines Peter Porter as an Athenian, that is, as a member of a repressive cultural élite. For Murray, Athens' hostility to Boeotia is a paradigm for the contempt of all subsequent empires, from the Roman to the British, for the simpler, traditional cultures of the people they conquer: 'Athens has recently oppressed Boeotia on a world scale, and has caused the creation all over the world of more or less Westernised native élites who often enthusiastically continue the oppression'. For Murray, the Euro-centred Australian 'native élite' is the worst and Porter is one of its chief culprits.

Behind his polite recognition of Porter's strengths as a poet – intelligence, skill, control of cadence – Murray's critique is oblique but devastating: that Porter has eagerly joined a metropolitan élite and adopted a style designed chiefly to oppress the reader; not just Australian readers, but all of us. This oppression is achieved by an insistence that only the past culture of Western Europe has value, and if we don't accept this, we are not worth speaking to.

Central to this is Porter's obsession with cultural references. He is often compared with Auden, but in this respect he is closer to Eliot and Pound, other emigrés to, not from, Europe. And he outdoes both of them. In this collection as in the previous ones, no poem is without cultural reference, literary quotation or allusion, usually several. But while Eliot and Pound used cultural reference to cope with their realisation that the European culture to which they had committed themselves was collapsing about them, no such anxiety perturbs Porter. His references signal obsessively, forty years on, that he has arrived from Brisbane and is at home in European culture.

What he cannot bring himself to accept is that this culture is no longer shared, that we are all Australians now. In *Millennial Fables,* however, the pretence of addressing an equally cultured readership begins to crack; the book ends, for the first time, with several pages of explanatory notes.

Porter's use of form and language is designed to give the same signal. Many of the poems in this collection are in rhymed forms – some taken openly from Marvell, Butler, Burns and Browning – which Porter executes with considerable skill. Others are unrhymed, but in precise, Audenesque forms. Throughout, there is a strong sense of form dominating content and of language used to brook no argument. Porter's characteristic mode is earnest generalising, with scant imagery, expressing some plangent regret on behalf of mankind. When he writes, for example, in 'The Grand Old Tunes of Liberalism' –

> All the great composers were heresiarchs
> of happiness. They believed in it in notes
> if not in lines, but a looking-out for votes
> converted their long melodies to simple quotes
> and Orpheus & Co's sound-bites in Sunday
> parks.

– the verse at first sight flows convincingly while the sense is deeply conservative, suggesting that the great composers were heretics (in fact, they wrote chiefly to commission) and that democracy ('the looking-out for votes') has diminished their work. On closer reading, 'They believed in it in notes / if not in lines' is clumsy and opaque, and the last line is incoherent: either it is an oddly dated reference to open-air concerts by municipal bands or it suggests that Orpheus is responsible for the pop music from transistor radios.

Like almost all the poems, this says nothing recognisable about the world in which I live. At a time when poetry's most urgent function is to give exemplars of joy and anguish, to share scarcely expressible feelings so that in our increasing isolation from each other we are not wholly alone, Porter produces bland, disengaged, Olympian performances expressing regret at the decline of Western culture. At bottom there is a frozen avoidance of feeling which is admitted in several poems, most notably in 'Connect Only' (get it?) which describes how a mentally defective man on an Italian train masturbated for hours against his wife's thigh and he did nothing.

There has always been a more relaxed, demotic strain in Porter's work, the other side of his obsession with culture and form, which appears here in a couple of prosy anecdotes ('Connect Only' and 'The Blonde Arm of Coincidence') and a whimsical fantasy about the end of the millennium ('Millennial Rococo') of which 'a regulatory body, OFFSOD / is created to monitor the cost of Rent Boys' is a fair sample. Porter has never shown the anger needed for effective satire.

The pleasures of this collection are occasional: the engagement with the messiness of creation in the first part of 'Aesop's Dressing Gown' and the voice of Bach's first wife, Maria Barbara, whose love of her husband is entwined with premonitions of her death, rendered to his music:

> He'll remarry
> and the published world renew its catalogue
> of wonders: choirboys will hang on notes
> like bells when my Exequien is rung...

Much of the poem has a magical quality of imagination and shows what Porter can achieve when he abandons received ideas and expresses feeling, even (or perhaps especially) through a persona. Here poet speaks to reader as an equal rather than posing as a wry world-weary academic. It is the direction in which Porter might remake himself, as Murray has done with his nature poems. Without such remaking, Murray's comment on Australian literature classes will apply equally to Porter's books, as 'places where people are sent to be humiliated'.

Pinch'd & Spooned

by Michael Horovitz

Allen Ginsberg,
Cosmopolitan Greetings,
Penguin, £7.99
ISBN 0 14 058736 5

The prattle of hype installations plugging poetry as 'the new rock 'n roll' and poetry readings as attaining 'unprecedented popularity' traduces a hard-earned living continuum. The facts are that 30 years ago, *before* rock concerts hit bingo, a cooperative of 16 beat, jazz, and sound poets headed by Allen Ginsberg, filled London's Albert Hall to overflowing; and that 40 years ago Ginsberg's *Howl* grabbed what then passed for poetry by the stiff of its collar, pulled off all its clothes, and brought the sullen art to communicative public life again.

Without these and allied impulses, Ginsberg's disciple Bob Dylan would never have reclaimed folksong from the shadows, or shouted '... even the President of th'United States/ sometimes must have/ to stand naked'. It's Ginsberg more than anyone who has sustained and replenished the confluence of transatlantic groupings, protests, liberation, music and song that's streamed between makers and listeners throughout these years.

The suggestion in Barry Miles's biography (*Ginsberg,* Viking, 1990) that 'he is perhaps least appreciated in Britain' has struck home again with some of the press for his latest volume, 120 pages of poems from 1986 to '92. He's been as highly regarded and affectionately befriended, as artist and person, by grass-roots communities across these shores, as he has everywhere else he and his work have reached. But what passes for criticism here, challenged by his continuing joy in the body's deep breaths and open forms, continues to close up and back away.

Douglas Dunn in the *Financial Times,* for example, misses the point in proposing that the new collection 'subtracts from his prestige as an icon of rhapsody by including an anti-smoking song. Lucky Kerouac, to have died before his talent and success drove him to give up fags and booze'. *LUCKY?* Kerouac's premature death from alcoholism was no more rhapsodic than those of Bix Beiderbecke or Dylan Thomas, or of Ken Tynan *et al* from nicotine addiction. It is Ginsberg's good fortune and natural intelligence that he's come to prefer cleansing the doors of his perception to stuffing them up: 'Smoking makes you cough,/You can't sing straight/You gargle on saliva/& vomit on your plate'. Or, as he put it in 'Maturity': 'Young I drank beer & vomited green bile/Older drank wine & vomited blood red/ Now I vomit air'. Would Dunn honestly regret it if Kerouac, Charlie Parker and all the other long gone icons of self-destructive genius were doing the same today?

It's ironic that a writer so often disparaged by little-Englandists for inartistic crudity, clumsiness, bad taste, formlessness, ignorance even, should be one who's so conspicuously helped us to (re)discover the meticulous craftsmanship of British minstrelsy, from medieval lyric and Campion through Smart and Blake to Bunting, Harry Fainlight, John Lennon. In a lot of rock you can't make out the words – and when you can, you may wish you hadn't! Ginsberg and those he's inspired or taught make a fine art of the text as a score for sounding, with each syllable, word or pause given its due weight and measure in the cadence.

The usually discerning John Lucas was provoked by Ginsberg's notation quoted on page 15 of the last *Poetry Review:* 'The girl at the counter, whose yellow Bouffant roots/grew black over her pinch'd face,/spooned her coffee ...' Lucas asks, 'if ÷pinch'd√ why not ÷spoon'd√? Isn't this a way of hoping to authenticate the inelegant by using precisely the kind of "poetic" strategy that someone concentrating on accurate observation should forgo?' Not at all: the elision of 'pinch'd' (ie, pronounce 'pincht') is a prosodic refinement that keeps the word short, as befits the rhythm of this subordinate clause, emphasising the girl's junk-taut features in passing, and lengthening the extra-slow monotone in which she 'spooned'. One is reminded of heroin habitually cooked up in spoons – as Thom Gunn remarked in the essay Lucas is criticising, 'her whole activity is summed up in the verb'. Such verisimilitude reinforced by perfect-pitch phrasing and auralisation is poetic indeed – no reductive quote-marks called for.

Ginsberg's calibre as a pioneer word musician is self-evident if one pays attention to his readings, performances and recordings. However: more than most poets I've read or known, he is constantly emptying his mind onto paper, and seems to take more and more pride in not editing the results. 'First thought, best thought' is repeated twice in *Cosmopolitan Greetings,* as it was in several previous books, and feels less convincing *qua* 'first thought' at each repetition.

It was not ever thus, as witness Barry Miles's giant format 200-page compilation *The Annotated 'Howl'* (Viking, 1989) – a tome only made possible because that work went through sundry drafts that incurred many second thoughts, most of them clear improvements (evidence their incorporation in the version Ginsberg published). The famous opening, for instance, 'I saw the best minds of my generation destroyed by madness, starving hysterical naked', originally read '... starving, mystical, naked'. Ginsberg later commented on this 'crucial revision': 'tho the initial idealistic impulse of the line went one way, afterthought noticed bathos & common sense dictated "hysteria"'. A still more exacting realism might have prompted the abandonment of 'best': of the minds Ginsberg has acknowledged as any kind of mentors he reckoned with, I can think only of Artaud, Pound, and his mother Naomi, as conceivably destroyed by madness. He's unlikely to have had these in his sights in *Howl* among those 'dragging themselves thru the negro streets at dawn looking for an angry fix'.

Four decades later he's become a poetry pop star and (anti-) Senator, and several of the polemical song lyrics and political raps in the new book, such as 'CIA/NSA Dope Calypso' or 'Numbers in U.S. File Cabinet' won't mean very much in a few years' time without extensive notes to disinter the ephemeral minutiae of their content. And not all the random reflections on who/what/ why he is ('Am I a Stalinist? A Capitalist? A/Bourgeois Stinker? A rotten Red?') or accounts of what/when/ how/with whom he's eaten/dreamed/slept/had sex, can be redeemed by his unflagging gifts for comedy, candour, vivacity and exhilarating pile-up of instantly recognisable sensuous detail. We have to thank our lucky stars for Ginsberg, but this side of idolatry, for all his palpable saintliness. I think of Ben Jonson's reaction to the legend that Shakespeare never altered a line: *Would he had blotted a thousand...* Given Ginsberg's vaunted – and to a great extent, proven – enlightenments through meditation, I can believe that he wants to 'write poetry because my head contains 10,000 thoughts'; but not that each one of these *is* poetry – let alone poetry worth publishing.

On the other hand, at least two-thirds of *Cosmopolitan Greetings* constitutes honest-to-goodness socio-spiritual teaching, hard-hitting humanistic prophecy and inspired verbal invention of a unique and invaluable order. Is there any poet in the West pushing 60, never mind 70 as Ginsberg is, who's gone on with comparable energy and commitment?

Thom Gunn concluded his ultra-sensitive review (reprinted in *Shelf Life*, Faber 1994) of the *Collected Poems* (Viking, 1985): '... It is *enjoyable*, informed by a continual honesty of intention and execution, and by aspirations toward ecstasy and vision that may recall to us earlier claims and prerogatives of poetry forgotten in the age of Larkin. It is the record of a career I find more exemplary with each succeeding year'. As do I – that much more so another ten years on. So let this glance at the new volume conclude with one of its characteristic improvisations, *Graphic Winces:*

In highschool when you crack your front tooth bending down too fast over the porcelain
    water fountain
or raise the tuna sandwich to your open mouth and a cockroach tickles your knuckle
or step off the kitchen cabinet ladder on the ball of your foot hear the piercing meow of a
    soft kitten
or sit on a rattling subway next the woman scratching sores on her legs, thick pus on her
    fingers
or put your tongue to a winter-frozen porch door, a layer of frightening white flesh sticks
    to the wooden frame –
or pinch your little baby boy's fat neck skin in the last teeth of his snowsuit zipper
or when you cross Route 85 the double yellow line's painted over a dead possum
or tip your stale party Budweiser on the windowsill to your lips, taste Marlboro butts
    floating top of the can –
or fighting on the second flight of the tenement push your younger sister down the
    marble stairs she bites her tongue in half, they have to sew it back in the hospital –
or at icebox grabbing the half-eaten Nestlé's Crunch a sliver of foil sparks on your back
    molar's silver filling
or playing dare in High School you fall legs split on opposite sides of a high iron spiked
    fence
or kicked in the Karate Dojo hear the sound like a cracked twig then feel a slow dull throb
    in your left forearm,
or tripping fall on the sidewalk & rip last weeks's scab off your left knee
You might grimace, a sharp breath from the solar plexus, chill spreading from shoulder
    blades and down the arms,
or you may wince, tingling twixt sphincter and scrotum a subtle electric discharge.

Raked-Out Coals

by Roger Garfitt

C.H. Sisson, *What and Who,* Carcanet, £7.95, ISBN 1 85754 068 9
Peter Levi, *The Rags of Time,* Anvil, £7.95, ISBN 0 85646 235 7
Thomas Lynch, *Grimalkin and Other Poems,* Cape Poetry, £7.00, ISBN 0 224 03973 3
Stuart Henson, *Ember Music,* Peterloo Poets, £6.95, ISBN 1 87147141 9
Neil Powell, *The Stones on Thorpeness Beach,* Carcanet, £7.95, ISBN1 85754 058 1
Neil Curry, *Walking to Santiago,* Enitharmon, £7.95, ISBN 1 870612 13 2

I once asked Charles Sisson what old age was like. 'Awful', he replied, 'I would have nothing to do with it if I were you'.

Reading *What and Who,* the collection which marks his eightieth birthday, I begin to see what he meant. It opens with a brief allegory, 'The Mendips'. An underground stream flows out of the mouth of a cave where, for a moment, imagination makes a 'single figure dancing in the shade,/ Naked as air, and it is she who slides/ Into the mind and eats the heart away. Turn back the spring/ which feeds the torrent... All is quiet now./ The eaten heart goes with it, and the man,/ Empty of grief as hope,/ Watches the sunlight on the glinting rocks'. Tranquillity, you might think. But that was turned back with the spring. No torrent, no tranquillity. What is left is nullity:

> Age has come again,
> And found its victim patient and at ease
> Upon a world that has no power to please.

Sisson has always acknowledged that poetic energy and sexual energy spring from the same source. 'Bring out your genitals and your theology', he wrote in 'A Letter to John Donne'. In these late poems he uncovers a further paradox: 'Beauty is a hunger, not a feast'. 'The Lack' he feels most keenly is the lack of desire.

Sisson explores this diminished territory with a relentless precision reminiscent of Samuel Beckett and, as in Beckett, the effect is paradoxical. Less becomes more by virtue of the courage with which it is explored. Age is seen for what it is, the last frontier.

Salvation comes with the discovery that 'Only a speechless look can be wise'. Sisson turns away from himself to 'the movement of the world'. *What and Who* may be his bleakest book but it is also, in a sense, his most celebratory. Nothing in his work is so tender or so delicately drawn as 'Figure' (female, of course). Even the poems that contemplate death directly, like 'Trees in a Mist' or 'Peat', have an austere beauty:

> The sum of everything would be the peat
> Which runs cool and dark between my fingers.
> It is night itself, a peaceful shower
> Which not one minute falls, not for one hour,
> But endures while consciousness lingers
> And follows it into its final retreat.

Peter Levi

One sadness of growing older is that you are surrounded by the shades of dead friends, those who succumbed early to illness or despair. Peter Levi published a set of three laments, *The Echoing Green,* in 1983, and a second set, *Shakespeare's Birthday,* in 1985. He has now added a third set and collected them all together as *The Rags of Time.* The new laments are for Nikos Stangos, the Greek poet, Constantine Trypanis, the Greek scholar and sometime Faber poet, and Elizabeth Frink, the sculptor.

Levi suggests that 'these lamentations' are 'more ragged and more raggedly felt than elegies'. What will strike the reader is the almost perfect balance between feeling and formal control, the intimacy of tone he sustains across an elaborate six-part structure. Only in the poems for Elizabeth Frink, a friend made late in life, is there the hint of a self-conscious exercise, of phrases being lifted from the clippings file.

There is a wonderfully supple use of the couplet, as in the final poem for Anne Pennington, which begins 'in river meadows' where 'the book of suns is too lazy to close' and ends:

> It is the image of your quietness;
> no one has ever troubled the light less,
> being so deep and so silent, as though
> a life lived is an hour in a meadow.

Even here, though, there are a couple of lines, 'and all of this, windshadow and birdbreath/ are somehow full of peacefulness and death', that are windy and shadowy in the wrong sense. One can imagine what a nimble satirist would do with 'birdbreath'. Levi is given to verbal patterns that do not mean much – 'George Herbert's green breath was a dying breath,/ green and white flowers sprout out of his death' – a fondness that intensifies when he comes to lament the world of shared beliefs that is passing away with his friends. He should remember what he wrote in his lament for Alasdair Clayre: 'nothing in life is boring but *grandeur*'.

Thomas Lynch

Thomas Lynch is an undertaker, brought up to the family business in a small town in Michigan. He discussed his profession in a recent article in *The London Review of Books*, a sensitive account that also touched on his predicament as a man left to bring up four small children on his own. The prose was laconic and beautifully turned. The poetry is more pungent. One can sense the angers that have been schooled into humour and compassion, giving each of these poems a firm rhythmic identity:

> one grave, one stone, one name on it, one rose,
> one fist to shake in the face of God then go.

He makes a sparing use of his mortuary material, reserving it for the occasional startling poem like 'That Scream if You Ever Hear It', and writes well of his own community, of his Catholic father with five heart bypasses, told to avoid 'sex with any but familiar partners', or the 'prim, widowed ladies from/ the Baptist Church in West Highland Township... their heavens furnished like parlours/ with crocheted doilies on the davenport... and God the Father nodding in His armchair/ at saints and angels who come and go/ with faces like neighbours and with names they know'. Inevitably, though, his job does set him apart, a feeling he has dramatised by inventing a persona, Argyle, the sin-eater, who moves through Lynch's ancestral County Clare in a past just this side of quaintness.

There is an inventive flyting of his ex-wife, marred only by a cheap crack about her making 'a fairly bouncy brain surgeon or well-dressed astronaut'. (What does Lynch propose to do in his mid forties? Become a chess grandmaster? A basketball star?) And some troubling sketches of the children of the divorce, 'settled into their perplexed routines'. What sustains the book are the glimpses of a difficult personal odyssey that brings him through to a second marriage and 'the one and only form of love / divisible by which I yet remain myself'.

His voice has grown like a late developing tenor – but not quite enough yet to carry him beyond that tricky middle ground where poetry can sound like crackerbarrel philosophy. The twang of a Country and Western guitar can just be heard in the background of 'Swallows' and 'These Things Happen in the Lives of Women'. Lynch is going to have to dig deeper into his own dark if he is not to end up as the Garrison Keillor of contemporary poetry. He could do worse, of course. But I suspect that he can also do better.

Stuart Henson

Don't let the old-fashioned title, *Ember Music*, put you off Stuart Henson's second collection. It deserves to be widely read. The best of these poems are fresh reworkings of timeless themes, as finely tuned as anything in John Burnside:

> ...the sky's blue is fragile,
> holy and cold,
> where the one star lifts
> like an aumbry lamp
> in that vault, in that emptiness.
>
> The horizon's pinks go rosy, go dim,
> a colour as thin as paraffin...
>
> While the planet hangs like a crucifix
> of acetylene
>
> on the night's brink.

He has a sharp ear for the music of mortality, hence 'the tin-foil threnody' of 'raked-out coals... in the hearth' – and an unusually acute perception of childhood as 'a grave and separate thing,/ Solemn like church, profound, soon to be gone'.

And yet that title does signal a real weakness. Henson is not so alert as Burnside to the problems of making a poem simultaneously ancient and modern. This is not a matter of living in rural Huntingdonshire, though some of his poems do seem to pass through a curious time-warp. 'The Newly-Weds' wash under a farmyard pump, only to drive home and put a record on the stereo. It is a matter of making it secondhand instead of making it new. 'It's the knave's luck and the poet's trick/ to stand in the right place at the right time' – but not if you are going to squander it by writing in the style of 1820. Henson comes on a sunlit oak in a frozen wood, 'a fountain pouring light'. And what does he do? Peer at it through a lorgnette, darkly, and see 'an infinity/ of glistered water-splinters in my sight'.

All the more of a waste when he can lift things right out of their time and place. 'Souvenir' and 'The Heron' are two of the best 'found' poems I know. It does not matter what their origins were. A newspaper report? An incident in the life of John Clare? They have been imaginatively transformed until every detail resonates.

Neil Powell

Neil Powell's formal verse is more accomplished than Henson's, but still not quite up to date:

While on the beach in random rows
The enigmatic stones compose
A silent staveless variation,
The music of regeneration.

Where would you say those lines came from? The Nineteen Forties? They are quoted on the back of *The Stones on Thorpeness Beach*, as if to establish its credentials, but what really make the book worth reading are its informalities, the risks Powell takes in writing directly of the vicissitudes of gay love:

And here's the blonde girl, perched on the landing,
Leaning on a sideboard I've never seen before.
'I told you he wasn't like that', she says, smiling.
'Oh, but' – I'm smiling too – 'he is. He is.'

The book is dedicated to the memory of the late Adam Johnson and there is an interplay between its different modes of address, between the confessional asides of 'True Stories', 'Anguishing by my Anglepoise lamp again,/ Waiting for open bars, open arms, open' and the skilful *vers de société* that describes a gathering in London of 'The brave and literate and queer', between the light tones of 'A Virus' with its heartbreaking glimpse of a lover who stops 'breakfasting on booze' and takes 'To healthy muesli, yoghurt, wholemeal bread,/ Storing up strength for the wasted days ahead' and the muffled Mahlerian kettledrums of 'Hundred River':

in one marbled, stained oak-leaf I sense gigantic change,
and in the drizzle feel the season fracture.

This seems to me music of a quite different order from that 'music of regeneration'. There is no sense of a predetermined shape being imposed, of something stamped out on a literary die-press. It emerges naturally from the observed detail of the poem, from the 'late scabbed blackberries' and the 'track of blackened railway-sleepers', the 'stealthy growth of fungus' and the 'hesitant leaf-drop'.

We come away from Neil Powell with the distinct sense of a personality. A little self-centred, perhaps, rather too ready to assume that the world is waiting to hear his desert island discs, but engaging, nonetheless, vulnerable and open to change. When he writes of a quiet evening with his lover, 'We are no longer locked in self-defence./ Being with you has made all the difference', we can tell what the difference is.

Neil Curry

That is what is missing from Neil Curry's second book. There are items of interest – Curry has a mind stocked with the curiosities of history and natural history – but nothing that makes a difference. These are eighteenth century observations, footnotes to Gilbert White. Only in 'the trumpet call/ of the asphodel' that ends a catalogue of the summer's flowers, 'the flower/ of Persephone, our Queen of Hell', is there the hint of a Johnsonian melancholy the observations may be keeping at bay.

Curry's first book, *Ships in Bottles*, was a much more purposeful collection. The curiosities had a point to them, an angry edge, and the long final poem, 'Alonso Quixano Encounters the Sea', was an inner as well as an outer journey. *Walking to Santiago* is neither. Curry walks the Pilgrim Road with his nose in the guidebook, regaling us with the Lives of the Saints. Apart from a couple of humorous encounters with Spanish peasants and one evocation of 'a long quiet walk over the meseta', he might as well be in the library. Which would be fine if he were searching his way towards Compostela. But there is no inner turmoil either, none of that depth of self-questioning that made Heaney's *Station Island* such a memorable circuit. The most Curry can manage is a diffident honesty, a rueful recognition of this sequence's limitations:

Maybe I've brought too much: guide books and maps
Can blur the edge of our uncertainties.
Travelling on with a trust in what was there,
They walked their faith. I walk their elegy.

CAROL RUMENS
The Planter's Epic

I

When I first heard her voice with its under-swell
Of a child's gruff lullaby to itself,
My heart undid like an old-fashioned pillow,
I could no longer speak
English as she is spoke in the Fatherland.
Rhotic abeyances, spurned vowels,
The stammerer's curse against the silencer,
Were charmed into surely ever-renewable
Volumes from her wood-sweet Linen Hall,
Our names twinned and carved in their secret spines.

One affricative could have held me
Like a sea never meeting, always surpassing
The lip of the shore, like a Russian abstract noun
Wiping the ache from its forehead with a soft-sign.
If her eye had said, 'Brit' or 'tart', my boat would have danced
On its curly-leaved ancestors
And havened safe in any wind of Antrim.

II

Her courtesies merely proved me the enemy.
Now the keel of my tongue is split,
And the brow of my spade batters rock
In the land she gave me with one hand, took with the other
– True son of my cut-throat heart.

I draw on this, my last imperial art:
The shutting-up of poets.
But the leaves I kill at night are clay tomorrow
In my cold engine-room, still readable,
Making me doubt what happens
To human texts when they are deconstructed
Even in the fiercest temperatures.

And I draw on myself, but it's sketchy,
A few red crossings-out while tuning in
To Radio Somerset, and the bath-taps whistle
The best-loved ditties of *Failte Isteach.*
Smarting, harboured, much of me vanishes. Home
At last! a bed of thorns. A froth of roses.
Sip me, foam, whisper your nothings, sweeter
Than any west of hers, much less a
Bare-faced lie than mine.

Notes:* Failte Isteach *is a radio request programme for Irish emigrants. The characters in this poem are purely allegorical, both being personifications of aspects (dialects) of a language.

Colonialism by Proxy

by Sean O'Brien

Edna Longley,
The Living Stream: Literature And Revisionism In Ireland,
Bloodaxe, £9.95
ISBN 1 85224 217 5

Edna Longley's *The Living Stream: Literature and Revisionism* in Ireland is an absorbing and infuriating book. It sends the reader back to Irish poetry with a freshened interest, but its habitual censoriousness seems mean in comparison with the art it sometimes brilliantly commends. Given its insistence on the health of diversity and the need for proper acknowledgement of the Protestant contribution to Irish literature, it is itself remarkably intolerant, at times managing to make its own professed reasonableness sound fanatical. It grows wearisome, for instance to be told again and again that Heaney is wrong – about Yeats, about Hardy, about History, about pretty well everything. Maybe he just differs. Fuelled by contempt for Irish Nationalism, *The Living Stream* is (despite a claim to the contrary) at the very least accommodating towards Unionism. It abhors narrowly national views, but God help any foreigner who dares to comment, especially if his name is Terry Eagleton. I'm not sure if pluralist zealotry is really possible, or if that is what Longley is really about. Occasionally there is the feeling that the poets may have so far outstripped the professors as to need bringing to heel. But at least Longley is *interested* in poetry.

For at heart, the book does seek to serve the power of poetry (even if the professor intends to be the final arbiter of where it resides), here valued for its capacity to live with flux and contradiction, to get beyond slogans and address complexity. As would be expected with Longley at the helm, Louis MacNeice figures prominently as a figure with the required gifts of flexibility. Longley is an effective user of quotation, and bits of MacNeice that may have seemed workaday are newly illuminated by her attention. Her readings of a variety of poets including Heaney, Mahon, Carson, Muldoon, McGuckian and Durcan also serve as a reminder that academic writing can serve purposes other than its own perpetuation. She does, for instance, a lot to commend Mahon's post-*Snow Party* work to those (including this reader) who have found it disappointing. 'No More Poems About Paintings?' contains her most exciting close reading, but the essays in literary history (for example 'Progressive Bookmen: Left Wing Politics and Ulster Writers') and the symbolism of Nationalism ('From Cathleen to Anorexia') are equally interesting, although Longley often works better over a couple of pages than the length of an essay.

If *The Living Stream* is a book which readers might find themselves hurling across the room, they are equally likely to go and pick it up again, and then hurl it some more, and so on. The long introductory essay, 'Revising Irish Literature', will probably prove to be the most provoking, even to readers sympathetic to Longley's case. Here she undertakes a revisionist campaign against the exponents of Nationalism – in particular Seamus Deane, the general editor of the *Field Day Anthology*. One point of attack is Deane's wish to be rid of acquired and limiting conceptions of Irishness while replacing them with what Longley argues is merely the same thing shifted to the textual plane. Deane, she insists, 'tries to have his Nationalist history and eat it, to deconstruct and canonise in the same gesture'. She has some deft fun too, with the rather notional Irelands described by Fredric Jameson and Edward Said, though her own considerations of problems of value and ethics are too brief for the context.

When the argument moves on to colonialism, Longley's performance suggests, a little surprisingly, that she's been a loss to that strain in English conservative thought which deals with opponents by denying them admission to the argument. Her proposal that the term 'colonialism' is inapplicable to England's treatment of Ireland leads to a view of John Hewitt's (no Fenian he) poems 'The Colony' and 'Colonial Consequences', according to which 'the power dynamics which these poems explore and exemplify – centring on land, religion, culture, and the locus of authority – play out the tensions between province and capital, ethnically troubled region and seats of government (compare Transylvania), as much as between distant metropolis and colony'. So that's all right, then. Despite his titles, Hewitt can't have meant 'colony', while the fact that colonies and provinces have problems in common means, somehow, that Ireland was not a colony. From this, one might infer that Britain never had an empire, just a hermeneutic blip lasting several centuries. The kicker, though, is that Longley entertains and then discards for the wrong reason, the idea that Unionist Ulster may in fact qualify as a colony, given the way, in the words she quotes from John Wilson Foster, 'the Ulster Protestant, feeling the perpetual threat of being taken over, already experiences in some sense, and exhibits the symptoms of, *the condition of being colonised*'. Perhaps this is an example of having your cake and eating someone else's.

While Longley introduces the essay with a brief account of her own mixed background – Catholic father, Protestant mother, Anglican compromise – she betrays no sense that her own relative privilege as the daughter of a professor at (then largely Protestant) Trinity College, Dublin might colour her view of the oppressive marginalization of the Protestant minority in the Republic. Nor does she acknowledge that the people she finds maddening might themselves be vexed by history and happen, having their reasons as she has hers, to view it differently, without being fools or psychopaths or liars. Of course her concern to show that literature can best engage with politics by the exercise of live intelligence and imagination is heartening, but Seamus Heaney, the frequent object of her displeasure, would say the same thing, and isn't it the case that by her account of Heaney's 'Requiem for the Croppies', this most literary of poets is tainted by the Popery that remakes Nationalism in its own image? R. F. Foster, addressing the problem of evidence in his chapter on the Famine in *Modern Ireland 1600-1972*, quotes Thackeray's *Irish Sketch Book:* '÷To have an opinion about Ireland√, one must begin by getting at the truth; and where is it to be had in the country? Or rather, there are two truths, the Catholic truth and the Protestant truth... Belief is made a party business'. Nobody, that is to say, is able to exit from the stage of history: what surely needs to be attempted is an examination of one's own prejudices. Longley doesn't seem to feel that she has any, but parts of *The Living Stream* seem written with one red hand behind her back. In the concluding section of 'From Cathleen to Anorexia: The Breakdown of Irelands', which is perhaps the most fascinating of the essays, she states: 'I have argued that Nationalism and Unionism are dying ideologies'. In fact the weight of her attention falls on Nationalism, and there is a weird comic passage where we learn that some ideologies are more ideological (and some consciousness falser) than others:

> Unionism does not linger like bog-mist in unsuspected crannies. For better or worse, you generally know it's there. Unionism exposes its contradictions in public: in the gap between its interior monologue and what it can get the rest of the world to believe. All ideologies work through unconscious assumptions as well as conscious creeds. But the Unionist unconscious, in both its secular and religious versions, has never been open to outsiders, whereas the reflexes of the Nationalist unconscious have been widely accepted as norms. The situation in the North is not helped by the tendency of Nationalist Ireland to reimport its own dated propaganda.

Ordinary dacent upfront bigots please form a queue. A critic sharing Longley's short way with dissent might point out that an English person referring to 'bog-mist' in this context would be considered racist. This failure of tone makes it unsurprising that Longley does not address the fact that however much the Nationalist and the Unionist hate each other, the hatred of the English for the both of them far outstrips their resources of rancour. Furthermore, the English make no nice distinction between them. The man on the Clapham omnibus, who is not reading Louis MacNeice or Paul Muldoon or much of anything else, considers them all to be effing Micks who while at liberty to blow each other's heads off should leave Our Boys alone. Perhaps he too may feel the condition of being colonised?

Art Critic Man Woman

by David Kennedy

Deborah Randall,
White Eyes, Dark Ages
Bloodaxe Books, £5.95
ISBN 1 85224 222 1

Deborah Randall's *White Eyes, Dark Ages* was published in 1993 and seems to have gone largely unnoticed so I'm grateful to the Editor for the opportunity to redress that state of affairs. *White Eyes, Dark Ages* is an imaginative exploration of the life and mind of John Ruskin through his relationships with the women in his life. Randall is clearly fascinated by the disparities between, for example, Ruskin's emotional petrification and his deeply felt responses to art; and between his sexual impotence and the fact that his most significant relationships were with women. The problem is that, like most people, I'm not a Ruskin expert and had to use *Britannica* to supply a biographical background without which many of the poems were puzzling. Similarly, I felt that many of the poems Randall puts into the minds of Ruskin and his women were too slight and/or oblique to communicate much about the characters or to work as poems in their own right:

He keeps her between two slices of gold,
A sandwich
Totally inedible.
'Her Letter'

Where Randall does succeed is in portraying the emotional trajectory of Ruskin's life, which if not exactly tragic is genuinely pathetic; and in longer poems such as 'You Do Not Know My Life' or 'Serpent In The Garden'. In these pieces Randall's pleasure in language is allowed full rein. I feel *White Eyes, Dark Ages* would have benefitted from greater emphasis on the connection between Ruskin's inner life and his aesthetics. An opportunity was also missed to examine his true relevance to the modern age in terms of his attacks on the social consequences of *laissez faire* economics. Ultimately, though, Randall's book is a creditable attempt at revaluation.

JOHN GOHORRY
Hokusai: Travelling around the waterfall country

In the waterfall country, a syllable glides to the rim
of a precipice and then falls in immense declarations
you attend to without respite and without dictionaries.

You carefully raise a glass, or your brush executes
deliberate representations. Beside them, the cataract
thunders down, magnificent and inexhaustible.

You draw near to the steady roar of the waterfall.
You contemplate for an hour, admiring its grandeur.
You have lived well until now in the divisible world.

The waterfall is the traveller imagining free fall
between summit and foot, and yet qualified,
as the fall itself is, by the pull of his object.

Between one waterfall and the next you compose verses.
On the road between memory and anticipation
the song of the distant falls as you reach for a cadence.

Few may ascend beyond the sixth waterfall.
At the eighth, there are carp moving in great shoals.
Life is an aspiration to this contentment.

Reviewers Reviewed

Dear Peter,

Laurie Smith's review of Vernon Scannell in *Poetry Review*, Vol 84 No 4 is a tawdry piece of writing. And this in an issue devoted to the art of reviewing!

Smith delineates Scannell's main themes, as he sees them, in a disappointing tone, and concludes with a bit of reductive amateur psychoanalysis. 'I'm interested in why people write poetry as much as how', he says. Exactly. Such a 'review' is unworthy of a literary journal: it is an inadequate treatment of 43 years of poems from one of our more distinguished senior poets.

Incidentally, as Smith is more interested in analysing poets than reading poems, I can recommend Scannell's enjoyable autobiographical volume *The Tiger and The Rose.*

Yours sincerely
Nigel Prentice
Coventry

Dear Peter,

The review of Vernon Scannell's *Collected Poems* in the recent *Poetry Review* contains pseudo-psychology of the most ignorant and dangerous kind. I am appalled that any Editor of repute should allow such stuff to be printed in the Journal of the Poetry Society, by a 'reviewer' whose only claim to fame is that he was once at school with John Major and is now a 'self-employed Educational Consultant' whatever that may be?

I have been including the poetry of Vernon Scannell in readings spanning a quarter of a century – (with his kind permission I hasten to add) – and it has never failed to engage, amuse, intrigue and move audiences of all ages and all persuasions. Would that just a few of today's overhyped, overpraised and over-indulgent 'poets' possessed one quarter of Scannell's talent and undeniable craft.

Truly Jonathan Swift was right in his assessment of the poetic scene, and I trust Scannell will brush off this grubby little flea with no difficulty.

Best wishes
Betty Mulcahy
Brighton
(Laurie Smith's credentials are, of course, his fine work for *Magma* magazine. – Ed.)

Dear Peter,

I was dismayed by Don Paterson's rather mean-spirited and condescending review of Norman Nicholson's *Collected Poems.* One of the functions of critics these days seems to be to piss on the graves of the not-long-buried.

The charge of provincialism (usually a limp metropolitan prejudice) against Nicholson is disgracefully old hat and to find it resurrected in the pages of *Poetry Review* and confirmed there suggests a policy of thinking reviewers more important than what they review ... after all, it is Paterson's aim to make sure poetry doesn't flourish unchecked! As far as provincialism is concerned, let's remember Douglas Dunn's '... what's wrong with love's / Preferred coutry, the light, water and sky / Around a town?'

If Don Paterson is short-circuiting the critical process then I can only think that in this case he has put all the lights out. Sure, mediocre poetry is more pernicious than bad poetry but I strongly disagree that Nicholson is as limited a poet as Paterson declares him to be. To celebrate the regional is not at all the same as being – in Paterson's wearily pejorative word – provincial. Unable to see the geological/cosmic levels in Nicholson's work, Paterson missed the universal in what is a considerable poetic achievement, and his post-modern cynicism makes him insultingly confuse religion with religiosity. It is Nicholson's Christianity (whether we approve of it or not) which explains why he sees the world differently and writes differently about it, differently from the way Paterson would like him to have written ... which says more about Paterson (who in any case seems to have tin ears) than it does about Nicholson ... but surely that was the point of the review?

Yours,
Matt Simpson
Liverpool

Dear Peter,

In the face of Don Paterson's confident assertion that Norman Nicholson's *Rock Face* was 'a widely acknowledged turkey', perhaps I should tell the story Norman told me, of his first meeting with Ted Hughes. Norman had been nervous of the encounter, not sure how he would be received. He need not have worried. Ted enfolded him in a great bear hug and told him how much *Rock Face* had meant to him.

Yours sincerely,
Roger Garfitt
Bettws-y-Crwyn
Shropshire

Dear Peter Forbes,

Don Paterson is a refreshing and entertaining poet but his reviewing is suspect. In a review of Norman Nicholson's *Collected Poems* he writes about Nicholson's misplaced 'short stresses' and his lack of 'redactorial' skills.

There is no such thing as a 'short stress' and it is a mistake to confuse metrical and stressed lines. Unlike a vowel or a syllable, a stress does not have length, and in the poem 'Egremont' which he singles out for criticism, the lines are stressed rather than metrical, so it makes no sense to speak of this poem as 'metrically challenged', whatever that means.

As for the word 'redactorial' – surely an ugly enough word in itself – the correct adjective from 'redact' is 'redactional'. Instead of coining such monsters, why not choose a less esoteric vocabulary? Such additional terms as 'metonymic resonance' tend in his review to obscure rather than clarify, although what he is trying to say in that context is not without interest.

Obviously, Paterson has a temperamental disaffinity with Norman Nicholson and I think I can see why. But his case lacks objective conviction. Those of us who like Nicholson's poetry are bolstered by the judgement of T. S. Eliot who found him a place in what was then the leading poetry list of its time.

Times have changed, but irresponsible criticism needs correction. There are some of us out here who could not only make a better job of reviewing poetry but would be glad of the fee for doing so. If Don Paterson thinks so little of Norman Nicholson, I would willingly pay him £10 for a book of poems I would love to possess but cannot afford.

Yours sincerely,
Michael Cullup
Wymondham

Dear Peter Forbes,

Really, Don Paterson should not have been given Norman Nicholson's *Collected* to review. As a poet himself he is still at the stage of setting off fireworks to see how they fizz and bang. How could he possibly be expected to appreciate a poet whose lifetime's acheivement was to express a democratic vision of a community and its locality. Nicholson had in abundance a quality that Paterson can only yet aspire to – Maturity.

Yours sincerely,
John Killick
Hebden Bridge

Dear Peter,

Peter Levi's review of Lydia Chukovskaya's *The Akhmatova Journals 1938-1941* contained a number of serious errors. The main points are these:

1. '...this edition of what seems to be the corrected and authentic record'. No 'seems' about it! This is the corrected and authentic record, as is clearly stated in the publisher's blurb, the details of the various editions being given on the copyright page.

2. Far from being ill-organized, the book is carefully, not to say strictly organized, though it is true to say that it is shaped by the circumstances in which it was created. First comes the preface to explain the context in which the diaries were written. Then come the diaries themselves with footnotes giving essential information, followed by those of Akhmatova's poems to which reference is made, then come the numbered endnotes giving detailed background information – all these comprise the author's 'text' – and lastly come the publisher's glossary and the index.

3. The first volume of the *Journals* was written in code during the Terror and the early years of World War II. It was decoded in the 1960s exactly as it has been written down, and subsequently subjected to a continual process of annotation, as each piece of information about the vanished past was brought to light. If you read the diary using the apparatus provided, not only can the 'vigorous immediacy' of the diary (Peter Levi's felicitous phrase) be appreciated but so also can Lydia Chukovskaya's feat of memory. It is remarkable that it was only the occasional initial that the author could not remember in the 1960s and that has remained elusive since. And because memory is a moral duty, Lydia Chukovskaya does not obscure these rare lapses but says straight out, as Mr Levi unreasonably objects, that she cannot remember whose name was protected by an initial.

4. The statement 'By Russian convention W.S. and K.G. turn out to be the same person' contains a misleading misprint (possibly not Mr Levi's): W.S. should read N.S., that is Nikolay Stepanovich (Gumilyov), who is the same as Kolya (diminutive of Nikolay) Gumilyov. Fortunately, readers more alert than your reviewer will be saved from confusion by the author's footnotes, which make this clear (see, for example, pp. 21, 89, 97 etc.).

5. The publishers, working with the translators, have been more helpful than Mr Levi allows: 'hazelhens' and 'ellipsis' can both be found in the *OED* and *Collins English Dictionary* while *'zaum'* (transrational language), *'Obllit'* (Regional Office of Literary Censorship) and the People's Will (a populist revolutionary organization) are all fully explained, along with a great many other references and acronyms, in the glossary. This was devised by the publishers precisely for general readers 'not entirely familiar with Russian nomenclature, literature or institutions'. However, 'Fedka the Eunuch' defeated us and remains, to our regret, unexplained; any information about this gentleman would be gratefully received.

6. The 54 poems by Anna Akhmatova were not translated by Peter France, as stated by Mr Levi, but by Peter Norman, who worked closely with Lydia Chukovskaya to produce clear English versions that would carry not just the meaning of the originals but also an echo of their form and tone. This appendix contains, in Lydia Chukovskaya's own words, 'those [poems] without which my entries would be hard to understand'; it is not wise, therefore, to follow Mr Levi's advice that 'this appendix is best ignored, or set aside to be read later'.

7. The three volumes of *The Akhmatova Journals* will certainly not be revised into one (which would amount, incidentally, to some 1000 pages) and certainly not on Mr Levi's less than competent say-so. Volumes II and III will be published exactly as their author intended.

8. Like much Russian fiction, Lydia Chukovskaya's two novels have been available in Russian in university libraries in Oxford and London and in other university libraries since the sixties, and in English translation as follows: *Sofia Petrovna* Barrie & Rockcliff, 1967; new trans. David Floyd, Harvill Paperbacks, 1990); *The Deserted House* (trans. Peter Norman, Barrie & Jenkins, 1972; re-issue forthcoming from Harvill). Chukovskaya's poetry has not been translated into English.

It is important for readers who may have carried away a false impression of this English edition to be aware that these faults Mr Levi finds with a book he otherwise praises exist only in his own inaccurate reading.

Akhmatova was a remarkable woman, and so is her great friend and memoirist Lydia Chukovskaya. Akhmatova would have been and Chukovskaya will be vexed (but unsurprised, I fear) by the carelessness of this review, and appalled at the reviewer's self-congratulatory remarks about the 'fun' of firing his critical 'pea-shooter'.

Yours sincerely
Bill Swainson,
Senior Editor, Harvill

Dear Peter,

As a reviewer of longer standing than any of the chosen contributors, I enjoyed your 'Reviewer' feature, but must point out that Blake Morrison's remarks are misleading. He says 'poetry is at least there in newspapers, as it wasn't before'. Too bad he wasn't around, or paying attention, earlier. Way back in the fifties, both *The Glasgow Herald* and *The Scotsman* managed to squeeze in new poems in space allowed. But by 1963 *The Yorkshire Post* led the field for consistent coverage of poetry, both in reviews and its regular Saturday Poem which took priority over adverts and journalism to the fury of the man charged with fitting its page together. During the three years of its reign, contributors included R. S. Thomas, Peter Redgrove, Richard Eberhart, Vernon Scannell, Geoffrey Holloway, F. Pratt Green, Norman MacCaig, and William Plomer. Two hardback anthologies culled many of these for later reprinting.

Your own editorial comments on the fact that few people are able to devote serious time to reviewing. You might weigh against that truth, that harassed editors somehow forget these reliable meeters-of-deadlines in their hurry to further burden the recently-successful ones juggling stints as judges with workshops, Arvon courses, interviews and half-finished novels when they are not doing the rounds of festival readings.

All the best,
Bill Turner
Lincoln

Seven Virtues

Dear Peter,

As a reviewer for *Outposts* and *Iron,* I would like to congratulate John Greening on his very eloquent attempt to encompass what poetry is about within 'Seven Virtues'. What a feat! The magic number seven. But only seven? Never. It's both impossible and appalling to think the muse could ever be so bound and gagged. Poetry is whatever anyone wants to say that is charged with 'feeling'. We can 'do' poetry. When we don't 'do' it, we write it. Poetry may well have its origins in song, and rightly so, but valuable poetic inspiration ought never to be sacrificed to music. What has changed about poetry today is that, like everything else, it has been subjected to 'scientific method'. What is this? If it doesn't do what I want, then I don't buy it. Partners do it, children do it with their teachers, people try to do it with their countries, if they're lucky. It's about self-determination. And poetry has never been so free! Free verse freed it. An age of science elbowed its way in and logic, rationality, genuine, uncontrived thought at its sharpest point does not lend itself easily to rhythms, metres and cadences.

Armitage is not 'merely' doing anything other people did. He is a highly original thinker with a new and clever delivery. There is always 'a crack' in his poetry through which the human glimmers, put it to music if you will. He uses shock tactics and negotiates his message – sometimes you must find the lyrics yourself. Listen carefully. He is a free thinker and a poet with remarkable energy. He is like the incredible hulk in the growth of his poetic appreciation and understanding – heaven knows what he'll be producing in ten year's time.

Like Kathleen Jamie says, it's the self we should hold on to. Children have it, any teacher will tell you that. And it's never artificial or self-conscious. This sets in later at secondary level when they learn that there is something they are supposed to think or do, and as Michael Caine says in *Educating Rita,* they learn to 'do the exam'. It's the weird pulling along a groove that we think we're supposed to be in that twists human nature and can make it 'more bestial than we could have conceived'.

R.S. Peters, the philosopher, has seen human emotions as conceptually based, and because of this there is any amount of possibility for supposedly educating them. Even into the art of torture. What is wrong is the commandeering of what people feel, or want to do, and taking away ownership. This is happening. Already we are being told we can't use this word, or that phrase in poetry, such and such is out. Who says so? Who can tell us what poetry is, or what it is not, what words we may or may not use? They're still using 'gossamer' on packs of sheaths, and yet 'certain' books have the cheek to say I can't use it in a poem.

All things have their poetry. Let it be. Use whatever works, ideas you want. Hang on to Kathleen Jamie's philosophy. Keep hold of 'the self'. She's young, but by God she knows what she's talking about, and thank God she has made it. It was a privilege to review *The Queen of Sheba* for *Iron* magazine. And by the way, Frances Wilson brought out a beautiful collection of poems: *Close To Home,* Rockingham, 1993, which I reviewed for *Outposts.* You forgot to mention it.

Yours sincerely
Wendy Bardsley
Stockport

COMPETITION

Report on No. 31: Pocket Classics

We asked for compressed versions of classic stories and poems

Following our announcement of the end of the Competition in the last issue, the entry for this one and the response to our questionnaire suggest that it needs a breather rather than termination. We hope to announce something new in the Autumn. In the meantime, suggestions are welcome. *Writers' & Artists' Yearbooks* to the following:

Cycnus
consider Cycnus, Phaëthon's trick
a sweet young man, such a downy chick

Phaëthon, wild as most sons are
burned to a crisp in his father's car

his last few cinders fell in the river
Cycnus swore he'd weep there for ever

he whinged so long and he grew so wan
Zeus feathered his pecker and made him a
swan

(an outcome more than a little absurd
you can't pull fellas when you're dressed
as a bird)

now not even Leda dares give him the eye –
once cobbled, twice shy

Ivor C. Treby

The Oresteia
Paris has run off with Helen,
Menelaus wants the head of the felon;
All the Greeks get together
But delays with the weather
Cause problems for king Agamemnon.

To get wind from a favourable quarter,
They ask him to knock off his daughter;
Iphiginia is killed,
Greek sails are soon filled,
And the Trojans are put to the slaughter.

Clytemnestra is left back in Argos,
In the arms of her lover Aegisthus;
After a wait of ten years
Agamemnon appears
With Cassandra, his soothsaying mistress.

The king is betrayed by his wife,
Iphiginia is avenged with his life;
The Furies ordain
That the queen must be slain
So Orestes turns up with his knife.

Now Orestes must pay for his crime,
But he slips out of Argos in time;
Apollo's outwitted,
Orestes acquitted,
And the Furies retired, past their prime.

Bill Phillips

Pride And Prejudice
Don't misally yourself, Bingley,
proud Darcy said. *Rather live singly.*
But the lady thus spurned
had a sister who turned
Darcy's head. Darcy wed. So did Bingley.

Gerda Mayer

(Relatively) Unassisted

Alert readers will have noticed that Kevan Johnson's name does not appear on the masthead of this issue. Kevan, who had been involved with the magazine since 1989, first handling subscriptions at Central Books, then from summer '91 as Production Assistant and from Winter '92/'93 as Assistant Editor, left in January to develop his career. We are grateful for the fine work he did for the magazine, not least his own reviews. He will be writing for the *Review* from time to time. You can also catch him in the short reviews section of the *TLS*.

In future Martin Drewe, the Poetry Society's Publications Officer, will be assisting with production and Rachel Bourke, the Society's Information and Marketing Officer, will be handling subscriptions and advertising. We are grateful to Kathleen Teehan and Morag McRae for production assistance with this issue.

PR Questionnaire

There was an excellent response to our questionnaire mailed with the last issue. Further questionnaires are being inserted in to the bookshop copies this quarter. If you haven't received one and would like to, please send us an SAE. Analysis and the winning entries for Reviewing the *Review* will appear in the Autumn issue.